The
Natural Sales
Evolution

Your customers have evolved, have you?

natural training

The Natural Sales Evolution

Published 2013 by Compass Publishing

A catalogue record for this book is available from the British Library

ISBN 978-1-907308-22-2

Set by The Book Refinery Ltd
Printed in the United Kingdom by Berforts Information Press
Edited by Lyn Place

Contents

Foreword

Contributors to the Foreword section include both Neil Warren from Modern Selling, and Ben Turner from the ISMM.

NEIL WARREN – FOUNDER OF MODERN SELLING
An independent body for the UK sales profession

Why does the modern day sales professional NEED this book?

Well, let's start to answer this question with another question: What are the consequences of not reading this book?

Put simply, as a sales professional you'll get left behind. The world of buying has changed which means the world of selling has changed. As a sales professional you need this book to help you take the simple steps to adapting in today's environment.

While your competitors are taking all your prospects off your hands and you're missing sales targets left, right and centre, you'll be looking around wondering what on earth changed. Well, I can tell you right now what changed: everything. And that has been driven by the internet.

The internet, specifically the changes in the online business resources in the past three years, has re-written the rules and transformed the selling and buying environment. This is rivalling all sales revolutions that went before.

What we're seeing is a planet wide realignment of how people live, work and cooperate. Where you once needed to be physically based somewhere, today you're not tied down by those same restrictions. What's more, the internet has liberated the buyer too. They don't wait at home for a sales person to knock on the door if they want to buy a hoover. They're empowered to go online and / or choose to take such research and go shopping, online or in-store – you've seen the adverts encouraging just that.

The modern day sales professional must take this seriously because the traditional methods simply don't make sense in the world we live in today. Why would they when there is a brand new platform that buyers and sellers are migrating towards?

Even if you are the best sales person in the world, nothing is staying still.

You need to keep changing adapting and evolving to make sure that you stay in the know and ahead of the game. Understand that everything is changing all the time, so read this book, evolve with the changes around you, and enjoy the financial fruits of your labour.

Neil Warren
MODERN SELLING
www.modernselling.com

BEN TURNER - THE INSTITUTE OF SALES & MARKETING MANAGEMENT (ISMM)
Also Founder of The SalesPro

There has been a fundamental shift in the way modern businesses conduct themselves. The evolution of social media and new technologies mixed with a larger macro shift in the world economy means that the way we sell today has changed, and with it, the nature of the sales professional.

Particularly over the last 24 months, the rise of the sales professional has been prominent.

The profession has further understood its value and its importance, and reflected on its poor reputation within business – the change has been realised and reacted to.

The sales professional is a different animal to that of the past 30 years. These individuals are knowledge-driven, have a deeper understanding of their environment and their client base, but perhaps more importantly, a deeper understanding of sales and what it takes to excel in this challenging profession.

As sales professionals assert themselves in the commercial world and seek new sources of information, new learning, and new knowledge, they gravitate to the best content and ideas that can help them increase performance – The Natural Sales Evolution is a prime example.

The *Natural Sales Evolution* encapsulates this change in the modern world and offers insight and expertise on how to handle and compete.

This book is a must read for any knowledge-driven salesperson; a must for any sales professional.

Ben Turner
ISMM & THE SALESPRO
www.ismm.co.uk

Introduction

"Skate where the puck's going – not where it's been."
WAYNE GRETSKY

We opened our doors at Natural Training in London in January 2005 which, at the time of writing, was nearly eight years ago. In that time we have trained 65,000 people in 2,650 companies, in 18 countries and 14 languages. Their attitudes, skills and knowledge have been diverse: there have been salespeople who were absolutely on a high after winning countless deals and making the most of their natural style, and salespeople who were at an all-time low, questioning their worth in a world that seemed pitted against them. And in between those two extremes there has been every type of selling attitude imaginable.

For all their diversity, the people we have trained shared one very important quality: they were mentally prepared to evolve and prosper.

It seems perfectly straightforward: we all know that customers are changing as the rhythm of business evolves. Likewise, we salespeople must evolve with them, or if we can, slightly before them. If we don't, we risk scrambling around for an increasingly smaller piece of the action. There is no doubt that selling has become tougher in the past few years. But this is only the case for those who haven't adapted their sales process and approach to suit the modern day buyer. This is EXACTLY what inspired us to write this book.

In our experience from this considerable sample of individuals, less than 10% evolve in an effective way to meet the changes of today. Those 10% of salespeople are in a very enjoyable position indeed, and don't really want the other 90% getting up to speed with today's natural selling evolution, because they are making great money!

So why don't salespeople evolve? There are several reasons – lack of motivation, energy, economic growth, successful management and plain old smarts being some of them. It also has a lot to do with attitude; As Wayne Gretsky says at the start of this chapter, it's much more common to chase the puck than predict its path. Likewise, in sales, doing the same predictable thing is easier than challenging tradition. However, just like in nature, it's not the strongest or most intelligent who survive, but those who are able to respond to the change around them.

The main opponent to sales evolution is fear. Salespeople carry with them some of the ritualistic attitude of top athletes: "If I win the biggest game of the year with my blue underwear, then I'm wearing blue underwear for every game." And the sales version: "If I win a big deal by presenting using PowerPoint, then I must present using PowerPoint for every big deal." (Never mind that the big deal was 18 months ago!) That's a sad indictment on a profession known for being goal-oriented 'go getters'. Fear of failure is, therefore, a bigger motivator for the majority of salespeople than the thrill of success.

Evolution in sales is about being strategically adventurous, bold and creative. It's about going for deals, and even if you lose, being remembered for being different. Better that than to lose and instantly be forgotten! Evolving in sales is also about being curious and picking up on the signs around you. If your customers are engaged in a new communication technology such as LiveChat, which is promoted on their website, then chances are you will establish a stronger connection by communicating with them using that technology. If customers are demanding value, then work out some ways to package it up and give it to them. And if customers want your solution to be different, stop saying "We can't" and start thinking about ways to adapt!

So, where does Natural Training, and this book, fit in with the fast changing selling evolution around us? Well, during the past eight years, we have helped salespeople to evolve by introducing them to a very personal, high-impact range of strategies and techniques that reflect two main dynamics:

1) How customers like to do business right NOW, and
2) The natural style of the salesperson.

Along the way, the results have been impressive in terms of our clients attracting and retaining the right type of clients, and closing more deals at higher margins – all with less work and anguish! We know we are on to something - which is why we published this book. It serves as a 'best-of' all of our techniques to ensure today's salespeople are better equipped to deal with change.

Do you have to make massive changes to be effective? Absolutely not.

Evolution starts with one small change that disrupts a pattern.

This leads to another change, and another, until it forms a

new pattern – temporarily completing an evolutionary cycle.

The key, however, is to make that first small change. Implementing just one or two of the tools and methods in this book will help drive your success to new levels. For example, while reading the first draft of this book for us, one of our clients noticed an idea that she hadn't realised could be achieved for such a low cost. She recognised that her sales team was communicating with customers in the same way it always had, which was having a negative impact. In fact, clients viewed it as dull and tiresome. So, she listened, and evolved the business to suit how the customer liked to communicate. As a result, in one month she moved from 20% conversion from pitching stage, to 50% conversion, which in monetary value was worth over £100,000. And that was just ONE of the techniques you are about to read. (We won't tell you exactly which one, but it appears in Chapter 13.)

The standout words in the example you've just read are: noticing, recognising, listening, evolving and, most of all, implementing! At Natural Training, we strongly believe that it's implementing what we teach that gets the results - not the theory. This is why this book is packed with practical advice and tips. Look out for 29 bonus sales tools, offers, templates and resources at the end of each chapter to help kick-start the implementation of your evolution strategies.

A final note on how to use this book...
It is not a novel that is meant to be read cover to cover, nor is it an instruction manual designed for robots. Instead, it is a rich breeding ground of ideas. We want you to read something so wonderful that your pulse starts to quicken, and your brain starts to whir. This book is designed for you to dip in and out of, as you prioritise your own issues.

As always, it starts with you. Where are the weak links in your sales cycle? For example, you might be fantastic at managing clients from online to offline (Chapter 11), but you feel you aren't describing your product in a way that creates excitement in today's market (Chapter 3). Or you might feel that you are up-to-date with modern objection handling techniques (Chapter 8), but you can't get hold of enough decision makers to begin with (Chapter 4). Or maybe you have no problem presenting to a client via some of today's newest methods (Chapter 7), but feel guilty about your poor LinkedIn presence (Chapter 12). The point is, work out what you need first and target that!

Make the book your own by scribbling notes all over it, personalising it to reflect your own natural style, feelings and goals. That way, it will be easier to own your evolution.

As always, we would be delighted to receive your feedback. If you would like to share your thoughts on how selling has changed, your greatest sales challenge, or about a current trend, please get in touch by calling our London office or emailing evolve@naturaltraining.com. I will personally see and hear about all of your communication.

Evolve and prosper!

Matt

Matt Drought
FOUNDER - NATURAL TRAINING
www.naturaltraining.com

Acknowledgements

JUST LIKE THE OPERATION OF ANY GREAT SALES COMPANY, PRODUCING THIS BOOK HAS BEEN A TEAM EFFORT. THIS BOOK IS A TRUE COLLABORATION WITH THE NATURAL TEAM OF COACHES, SALESPEOPLE AND DIRECTORS.

Selling runs through the blood of everyone in our team. Like you, we're passionate about sales and about getting results. We like to call ourselves 'The Naturals' because we're committed to providing you, the sales professional, with the latest strategies, techniques and tools to help you naturally evolve in this sales evolution. It made coming up with the title nice and simple: *The Natural Sales Evolution.*

The Natural team of contributors includes Fiona Challis, Nick Golding, Fred Robson, Deborah Sowry, Paul Owen, Paul James, Greg Keen, Mark Williams, Sean Sidney, Salli Glover, Pat Upton, James Marshall and Mark Fineman.

And to all our Naturals who could not contribute to this book but who have absolutely contributed to our success over the years, a massive thank you.

We would also like to say thank you to Ben Turner and Neil Warren for their forewords.

Thanks also to my wife and business partner, Feena, and our beautiful baby girl, Sive, who are both a constant inspiration.

I would also like to say thanks to our loyal customer base and subscription base for supporting us throughout the years and for welcoming us into their sales organisations.

Finally, we would like to dedicate this book to the sales profession. Salespeople get an awful kicking from all angles, and probably always will, but we box on with determination and pride.

THIS IS FOR YOU.

29 FREE SALES WORK KITS, TOOLS AND OFFERS WORTH £1,350!

At the end of each chapter, you will see some bonus resources to help kick-start your personal selling evolution.

HERE IS THE COMPLETE LIST:

1. Natural Sales Evolution Audit
2. Sales Maker worksheet
3. Customer Decision Making Cycle worksheet
4. 20% off our Complete Telesales Skills open workshop
5. Customer Personality Analysis worksheet
6. Value Selling Warren Buffet Style - PDF
7. Value Proposition Creator
8. Five tips to handle gatekeepers and leave voicemail – audio file
9. Send us your phone recording – free coaching offer
10. BITE PDF and template
11. Role Play template
12. NaturalFlow™ Questioning desktop planner
13. Case study template
14. Trusted Advisor tip sheet
15. 10 Tips for Client Video Testimonials
16. *The Winning Pitch* e-book download
17. Send us your video sales pitch
18. Get 20% off our Open NaturalStyle 2-Day Presentation Skills workshop
19. PURE Objection Handling worksheet
20. 50% off a Natural Training Objection Handling session

21. Negotiation Dashboard template
22. Procurement Profiler download
23. Secrets of Selling to Procurement – audio file
24. Procurement Matrix worksheet
25. One page Lead Generation Plan
26. *HEAT* e-book download
27. Free 'Online to Offline' marketing critique
28. Performance Mindset & Goal Setting planner
29. 21 Recommended Sales Resources factsheet

To access the Natural Training sales resource centre for your 29 FREE resources, simply register online at www.naturaltraining.com/bonusresources

Chapter 1 - How selling has evolved

"Good Evening Mr Bond"
THE QUEEN

Selling is evolving, and we must evolve with it. The time to change how we prospect, develop relationships and sell is NOW. This chapter looks at how selling has changed. We highlight what exactly has changed and what you, the sales professional, need to do to adapt and find the levels of success that you've been used to in the past...

They say that the Olympic Games don't really open until the flame is lit in the main stadium. However in 2012, many people felt that the real starting point of the London Olympic Games was signalled with the immortal words spoken by the Queen, "Good evening, Mr Bond".

Producer Danny Boyle had pulled off a master stroke: James Bond (played by Daniel Craig) walked into the Queen's actual private quarters and escorted her out of Buckingham Palace to the Olympic ceremony. It was unlikely – and it was magnificent!

Five years ago, if you asked anyone whether it would be possible for the Queen to embrace pop culture and do an acting gig with Daniel Craig, they would have laughed in your face. Now, having made this leap, it's not inconceivable that the Queen herself will be Tweeting on a daily basis in the near future. Watch this space!

The point is, that simple act by the Queen represented much more than a bit of fun. It represented real and exciting change – a significant milestone in the evolution of culture and communication. When you break it down further, it becomes even more exciting. Here is a figurehead, representing one of the most conservative and dignified organisations on earth, doing a cameo in a promotional piece by a producer who shot to notoriety with a film about a group of heroin users!

The real message is if the Queen can change, so can you. The way customers buy and salespeople sell is evolving.

The rules are evolving around us daily at a pace that's leaving many salespeople cut adrift.

If you work in sales, you need to sit up and pay close attention to what's happening around you. Sell how you have always sold, and you risk becoming a relic of the past. Embrace the new world of selling and you have a wondrous opportunity to be at the vanguard of sales success, enjoying the increased income as a result.

Let's have a look at the way selling has changed in the past five years: (See next page.)

What is driving this change at the moment?

In truth, there is only one main driver. It sits at the heart of the sale and is the real hero. No – it is not WHAT you are selling (yesterday's hero) but WHO you are selling to.

Insider Tip: Your customers are central to everything now because they are infinitely more educated and resourced. They make very powerful allies indeed!

Yesterday's selling	Selling NOW
1. Traditional selling approach	1. Blended selling approach
2. Product is King	2. Customer is King
3. Salesperson generates leads	3. Technology generates leads
4. Cold calling is weight of numbers	4. Develop modern, smart and intelligent cold call campaigns
5. Salespeople rely on customers knowing less than they do	5. Educated modern day buyers know more than some sales people!
6. The priority is on relationship selling	6. The priority is on providing value and results
7. There is no recognised power in Procurement function	7. Selling to Procurement and Buying Agencies is, in most cases, a necessity
8. "We have loyal customers who only spend with us."	8. Customers are constantly being tempted with competitive offerings and their spend is fragmented
9. "We communicate solely with customers by phone and face to face."	9. "We now communicate using multi-media platforms including Webex and Skype."
10. The sale starts with a call	10. The sale starts online
11. "I am a salesperson."	11. "I am a Sales Maker."
12. Salespeople qualify leads	12. Customers use an automated online sales process to do the pre-qualifying for you
13. "I don't need to change my sales approach because my results are fine."	13.You are missing out on a huge opportunity to improve your results. Going from being good to great is within your power but it takes the right attitude.

Modern day buyers have changed how and why they buy, which has created the need for the modern day sales professional to change how they prospect and sell.

So what has sparked this change?

We know that the entry of the internet marked a huge change in selling. In the last few years, however, the internet has evolved from being a graduate research assistant to a powerful consumer ally.

At the click of a mouse, your customer has a unique window into your virtual shop front. But that's just the start. They also have access to details about your people, your sales performance, your company records, your customer information and many other facts that will either work for you – or lose you the sale before it has even started. The information and choice available to buyers today gives them great buying power. And don't customers, as we all are, love it!

In many cases, a mildly interested customer is more informed than a lazy salesperson.

That's a key role reversal. The buyer can reach everything they need in an hour or two and have all sorts of buying advantages.

This means that the modern day sales professional not only has to adapt the way in which they sell, they also need to ensure that they know their industry, sector and products and services inside out.

HERE'S A GREAT EXAMPLE...

In 2008 at Natural Training, we did a few days of telesales training for a reseller of a major photocopier brand. The company's whole sales process involved cold calling schools, surgeries and small government agencies with the aim of selling them a photocopier for £13,000 with a large, ongoing maintenance contract. The company sold about a dozen of these machines a month. However, if its customers had simply 'Googled' the model number, they would have seen the same product for £6,200. That's right – the reseller's business model was reliant on 100% mark-ups from standard retail prices.

The customer, as always, was central to this. This company, which had 12 salespeople, was relying on an ignorant, poorly resourced customer base. It was a market the company desperately hoped wouldn't check or compare pricing; a market of trusting or non-caring customers who would have bought anything from anyone. In other words, it was a rapidly shrinking market. We had discussions with our client - begging the key decision makers to develop a more sustainable new business strategy that could initially sit alongside the shrinking one, and then take over in the long term. They didn't listen.

Fast-forward to 2012 and that same company only has two employees – the Director and the Administrator. They work out of the Director's lounge room. They are essentially washed up – finishing up the last of their maintenance contracts, wondering what went wrong (blaming the customer), and working out what to do next.

So, what happened in this example?

It's simple: technology evolved. The internet pulled their uneducated customer base into a position of wisdom. Their competitors also evolved, forming alliances with other organisations that were able to get them larger contracts in the new 'print solutions' space. Yet this company failed to evolve – applying four-year-old business practices to a market that no longer needed them.

Meanwhile, the rest of us realise that sales is evolving fast - led by a wise customer who is spoiled for choice. That customer wants to do business on their terms, be communicated with in the way they want, with their considerations met at every turn.

This educated customer is central to selling today. Successful salespeople and selling organisations have evolved their sales process to meet the market. These people aren't pushing their sales process onto a market that doesn't want it.

Customers need to be listened to, and they want to deal with people who want to develop and collaborate with them.

Put simply, today's buyers will not tolerate weak, ill-informed salespeople. Sales roles have changed over the years.

In the following diagram, (see next page) you can see the evolving nature of salespeople, from Seller to Sales Maker:

1. Seller: "I think I have what you need – now I need to convince you."
2. Consultant: "I'm going to ask questions to find out what you need."
3. Collaborator: "Let's work together to find out how we can make your life easier."

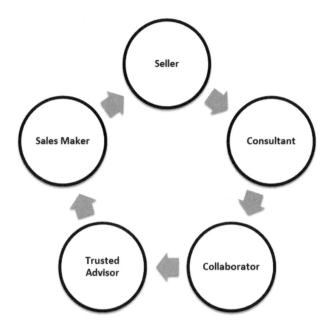

Figure 1.1: Sales Maker Evolution

4. Trusted Advisor: "You see me as the expert, so I'm going to encourage this trust with sound counsel and genuine empathy."
5. Sales Maker: "You know what you want and you need me to make it happen."

The salesperson now MAKE the sales happen by bridging the gap between computer and customer. Sales Makers are the face of the organisation. They bring the brochure to life, they personify the sales process, they fill in the warm, human component that technology cannot. They have the facts to hand. They don't oversell, or hard sell. They make you like them, and you want to buy from them. Simple.

Each part of this evolution is critical and valued. There is nothing wrong at all with being labelled a 'seller': people who sell make the world go round, and we need them more than anything. When I want to buy a Big Mac, I don't need a consultation. I want to hand over the money, and walk out with a hamburger.

The same principle applies to consultants, collaborators and trusted advisors: these are all very valuable roles that you make your own depending on your industry and where you are positioned with the customer.

It is the Sales Maker, however, that we would like to focus on, because we feel that this is the newest breed of salesperson.

WHY THE ROLE CHANGE?

First some background: as we discussed previously, your customer is at their most sophisticated right now. If, five years ago they were at a Bachelor Degree level, now they have attained their Masters in you, your company, your pricing and everything else they need to know. They may even have sampled your product, or talked to an existing customer, or filled out an enquiry form outlining exactly what they need. (In that enquiry form, it is getting increasingly common for customers to write, "Don't call me, I just want a price" or "This is an early stage – please no contact".)

Customers are used to dealing with a 'thing' (the internet) rather than a person, which is you. They are much more trusting of technology. In fact, as Gen Y (born 1980s to 2000s) moves into management, many don't know any other way.

They don't want to talk to anyone – they know what they want, and they get it.

For example, recently we were contacted by a genuine 'digital native' – a Gen Y Human Resources and Training Director from an office supply company with 92 employees. One of our salespeople took the call, and was surprised at the information the caller knew. For example, she knew more about two of our competitors than he did! She had three very quick, sharp questions:

1. How much is it for eight people to get trained in high value proposal writing?
2. Do you have availability on December 3?
3. Do you have a trainer with the right experience for our industry – it wasn't clear on your website?

Despite his best efforts to keep her on the line, the call was over in two minutes. She wouldn't give any particular contact details, nor would she entertain another call. Rightly or wrongly, she knew what she wanted, and our sales guy couldn't find a way to add any value right then. He did have her name, and was able to follow up later, but in many respects, he felt the horse had bolted. We never got the business.

This might strike you as an extreme example, or it might be happening to you frequently. Either way, it is definitely becoming a much greater part of today's Natural Selling Evolution. At Natural Training, we used to get a dozen calls like this every year. Five years on, we get two or three of them a week: that is, customers using the phone purely as a way to find stop-gap information and moving on quickly. They simply don't want engagement.

ENTER THE SALES MAKER!

The Sales Maker, as the name suggests, makes the sale happen. They are the human face of the company, the conduit between a computer screen and the delivery of the product. Simply stated, Sales Makers add the bits that an online experience can't provide.

Key attributes of a Sales Maker in today's selling evolution include:

- ✓ Sales Makers need to be 'Johnny on the spot': available right there, right away, within two to three rings of the phone.
- ✓ They need to be on their 'A game': the consultation time period has trended down quite substantially. If customers used to have 30 minutes to talk to a salesperson, today's new breed of customers have ten minutes.
- ✓ Sales Makers need to add value – a spark, something different and new that the internet hasn't provided their customer.
- ✓ They understand that the customer must be persuaded – quickly. They have to bring their considerable talents to the table in record time, and help structure a persuasive argument based on the customer's reality. Not easy, but achievable with practice and a dedication to the evolution!
- ✓ Sales Makers understand that customers are more guarded, because they don't want a team of rabid salespeople to set upon them. They will have their defence mechanisms up!
- ✓ They will use a phone conversation as a launching pad to other media, as they understand customers

will be open to being approached via LinkedIn, Skype and MSN Messenger.

✓ Sales Makers know today's evolved customers don't want to wait around for quotes, proposals and next steps. They know that customers see no reason why they can't have it NOW! And when they do get it, they don't want to wade through information to find out what they want. They aren't conditioned to search for stuff for longer than about ten seconds.

✓ Sales Makers know that one small step to undermine **trust** is deadly, particularly during this increasingly smaller window of contact.

If you recognise some or all of the above attributes, then the pressure is on! Welcome to the Natural Sales Evolution!

Does this mean that the role of the salesperson will become redundant?

The simple answer to that is, no. In 2000, around the time of the dotcom boom, some people predicted this would happen. Yet 12 years on, and sales professionals are thriving in most industries – even the ones that were definitely going to be redundant, such as travel. It seems that the human face of your commercial organisation, the salesperson, will always have a valuable role to play. However the role is definitely adapting at a rapid pace.

SO LET'S LOOK AT SOME OF THE OTHER MAJOR CHANGES...

Although we would love not to include the economic downturn in this book, we can't hide from the fact that it has been a major factor in how customers have changed their buying habits. We would like to stress, however, that salespeople who use the economic downturn as an excuse for not achieving are simply in denial of the new ways in which you can still successfully sell.

So how has it affected sales? Well, the major change is that a lot of companies made some cutbacks within their organisations to reduce costs and increase profits. This means that today's decision makers are more than likely to be in multiple roles with increased responsibility, which makes time their most precious commodity. This affects their ability to concentrate, to read sales and marketing collateral and to take sales calls or visits.

The economic climate has also had a major impact on the decision making process and budgets. In the business to business (B2B) arena, five years ago you might have sailed through the decision making process without having to go through Procurement. Those days are gone, and many decision makers are measured on how much money they save and the extra value they generate. We'll talk about this much more in Chapter 10, which is all about Procurement.

Buyers know that some salespeople will heavily discount simply to win the deal - putting them in the driving seat when it comes to getting the best price. They will know, for example, why you are particularly keen for them to buy off you towards the end of the month when your targets are looming!

Remember, today's customers are better equipped, educated and far more aware of salespeople needing to maintain existing accounts and win new business.

When you do finally get to engage with customers offline, you will be one of the chosen few that they have carefully selected to give you their precious time. With time being precious and the level of information they already have at hand, today's buyers are demanding. There is less tolerance for small talk and a greater desire to have you, Ms Sales Maker, get to know their situation efficiently and recommend the right solution.

They also won't tolerate seller-centric salespeople who simply want to talk about themselves – you need to have customer-centric messaging.

Buying has changed, and this has initiated the change in how we sell. Continue to sell as you have always done and you will miss out. Adapt and change your approach using the information in this book and you can look forward to getting back in the driving seat of your sales success.

So what particular skills do you need in the Natural Sales Evolution?

To be a Sales Maker, you need to convert calls and meetings into customers and sales. You need to have a strong value proposition. You need to ask intelligent questions that positions you with trust, credibility and nous. You need to be ready to prove results. You also need to be prepared to handle objections, have confidence in moving through the negotiation arena, and be ready to sell to Procurement.

These are must-have skills for the modern day sales professional which is why we have included a separate chapter on each of these skills in this book.

Summary

- If the Queen can evolve, so can you!
- Selling has changed in 13 fundamental ways over the past five years, which is mainly technology led.
- Today make the customer the hero – not your product.
- Customers have evolved to be much more educated and won't tolerate ill-informed salespeople.
- Salespeople have evolved, too. Today it's all about the Sales Maker – bringing a sale to life.
- A key skill of today's Sales Maker is making a rapid, favourable impression.

TIME TO EVOLVE! YOUR SALES TOOLKIT:

- Become aware of how you are currently selling by taking our natural sales evolution test. Find out how much of what you are doing from five years ago still works and how much you think needs to be changed.
- Download our FREE Sales Maker worksheet – perfect to help determine the type of profile you need in today's selling evolution.

To access the Natural Training sales resource centre for your 29 FREE resources, simply register online at www.naturaltraining.com/bonusresources

Chapter 2 - Understanding the modern day buyer

"It's choice, not chance, that determines your destiny."
Jean Nidetch

In Chapter 1, we established that selling has changed and how vitally important it is for the modern day sales professional to evolve with that change. Today's buyers have essentially changed the rules – particularly the 'how', 'why' and 'where' they buy. In this chapter, we look at the modern day buyer and help you to get inside the head of the type of buyers you will be targeting. Without this information, how can you possibly evolve your sales process and approach?

Let's start with an adage and 'walk a mile in your customer's shoes'. You see, to understand your customer you have to ask yourself a series of questions. Only then can you add value to them and sell effectively.

Take an example of a typical buyer or decision maker you deal with and answer the following questions:

1. What does an average day look like for them?
2. What are they saying, thinking or feeling?
3. What are their key objectives when buying?
4. What are their key business objectives and goals?
5. What challenges, issues or problems do they currently face?
6. What do they really want to achieve?

7. What changes have taken place within their industry, company or status that could affect their ability to make a decision to buy?
8. Are they under any time or budget pressures?
9. How do they measure success?
10. What will they need to achieve to see that buying your product or service has been a wise decision and is providing the Return on Investment (ROI) they wanted?
11. What are their greatest fears in making decisions?
12. What are the possible risks they could be concerned about?
13. What is their buying process?
14. Does your buyer have the autonomy to make a decision or do they have to involve others in the process? If the latter, who do they involve?

Asking yourself these questions and then answering them will help you to 'walk a mile in your customer's shoes' because you'll truly understand their perspective. You'll also be far closer to understanding the modern day buyer.

Key Question: Have customers changed in comparison with five or ten years ago?

Well, for the most part, yes, they have. Buyers and decision makers today are under immense pressure – this is normally driven by time and money constraints. Due to these pressures, buyers have less time for cold calls or spontaneous meetings. The decision makers you need to talk to are dedicated to key business priorities, meaning if buying your product or service isn't aligned to their goals and objectives, then you'll struggle to get their time.

Are your customers suffering from 'analysis paralysis'?

Time also affects the buyer's ability to concentrate. The customer wants to get things done as quickly as possible without missing any important information. Remember, most buyers today suffer from what we like to call 'analysis paralysis' - too much information overwhelms them. So keep it simple and to the point.

A lot of buyers who previously had the autonomy to make a decision alone are now forced to involve others in the process – people who will be privy to the analysis paralysis, too! What does this mean for you? Well, it means a longer and more complicated route to closing a deal. Today's buyer may also be scared of making a decision through fear of personal retribution. As a consequence, they will consider risks a lot more carefully, and will need to see proof of value and results before buying.

In the majority of cases, they will want to prove to others in the decision making team that they got the very best deal available.

Due to all of these pressures, they also subscribe to the 'If it ain't broke, don't fix it' philosophy, which means winning competitor business is a tough game. Unless you can demonstrate that it MUST be a business priority to switch to your product or service (because there is suitable value in doing so), it's going to be a real challenge.

The decision making process

Once you truly understand your buyer, your next step is to

understand the decision maker's buying process. Consider for a moment that there's a sudden role reversal, and you were the decision maker, as opposed to the seller. Get in their shoes for a second...what buying steps would you go through?

Based on our experience in dealing with today's decision makers, here's an example of key buying steps:

Figure 2.1: Customer Buying Cycle

1. Identify they have a need.
2. Research online.
3. Select a shortlist.
4. Engage with sellers offline.
5. Go through Procurement or decision making team.
6. Buy from a supplier they like, trust and feel they can work alongside.

Let's look at the research stage. If you believe that during a sales conversation, you automatically know more than the buyer, you have a traditional view of sales.

Ignore the knowledge of today's buyer at your peril! Usually the buyer is equipped with just as much information as you, so never underestimate their knowledge.

WHAT'S THE MAIN CONSEQUENCE OF MAKING THIS ASSUMPTION?

If you think you know more than the buyer, consider how you'll feel if you lose all credibility as a sales professional because you get caught out by the buyer's superior knowledge. Can you think of anything worse? A prospect asks you a question. You're caught off-guard but manage to respond with what you hope she will accept. But she doesn't. In fact, she catches you out and starts telling you about the products you sell. You've just taken 10 paces back from making the sale. And the customer is walking out the door.

Modern day buyers have arrived

And they don't have much time! They are pounding up and down the virtual high street at this very moment, searching for products on the internet. Dependent on the complexity of your offering, some buyers will complete the entire buying process online whilst others use it as a research tool to arm themselves with relevant information before contacting the seller.

Consider this modern buying cycle:

1. Visit coffee shop and buy coffee.
2. Drink coffee and log onto Wi-Fi via smartphone.

3. Search for product recommendations.
4. Assess product features and latest reviews.
5. Search for best possible price online and buy, or
6. Visit store armed with more knowledge than ever before.

When you think about it, often we (as customers) don't actually come face to face with the salesperson until we have to make a pretty important purchase.

In the same way that the recession has put salespeople under pressure to squeeze everything from encounters with the customer, technology exerts further pressure on the sale. Technology has effectively reduced the amount of time the salesperson gets to sell.

Customers will only have patience for those salespeople who can give them exactly what they need – there isn't any time to waste!

Key Question: If customers are time-sensitive, intolerant of poor service and demanding, how should selling strategies adjust to this trend so that they remain relevant?

Let's look again at the modern day decision makers' buying process. The first three steps are now happening online: Identify need, research online, and select a shortlist.

Online

It's the move from online to offline (you!) which is critical. (See next page for diagram.) In later chapters, we provide some great insights into exactly what information you should be displaying online to get to the opportunity to engage with more decision makers offline. We have also included information on how to be better equipped to provide customers with exactly what they want to see and how to navigate your way through the decision making process successfully, moving from being shortlisted to winning the deal.

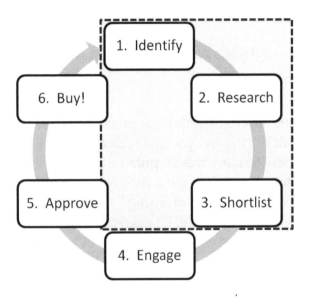

Figure 2.2: Customer buying cycle online influence – customers may not be on your radar until stage 4

Today's personality analysis

Buying and selling has changed. Gen Y buyers are in management, and they grew up with the technology that you are selling with and sometimes against.

Here is a simple personality analysis that will help you to be more aware of your buyers and, importantly, how to sell to them:

THE NATURAL SALES EVOLUTION

Figure 2.3: Buyer Personality Analysis

The Pulse Buyer

➲ **Personality:** Restless, aggressive, quick to click, and quicker to buy; you really need to be on your A-game to close this impulsive buyer.
➲ **They say:** "Give me a proposal by 3pm and I will let you know in the morning."
➲ **Selling to a Pulse:** Be assertive and confident. Be ready! Your window seems to be about three minutes! They will call you, having done their research, and they will be hot to buy.
➲ **Sales tip:** Sell the way they want to buy! Cut out meaningless steps, and have your close ready.

The Bloggy Buyer

➲ **Personality:** The type of buyer who loves to socialise and interact. They are chatty and like to see and feel your product. They will contribute to your blog and offline forums. They will be friendly and go off-topic – and like to talk about themselves!
➲ **They say:** "Let's have a meeting. I would like to introduce you to a few of my colleagues."
➲ **Selling to a Bloggy:** They like people so make

40

friends! Set aside some extra time to socialise. Be aware that they need to be focused back to the sale, if you are going to make a sale happen!

◌ **Sales tip:** You can go off-topic with them, but focus them back to your product with a favourable blog review, or invite them to 'join the conversation' and offer their opinion. They can even write something for your company, or be the hero of a case study.

The Luddite Buyer

◌ **Personality:** This buyer moves slowly. In fact, they are so far beyond the curve they are thinking of joining Facebook 'one day' and believe that Twitter is a Ronald Dahl book. So, you need to cater for this.

◌ **They say:** "I'm not sure we are ready yet."

◌ **Selling to a Luddite:** While sales has evolved for many people, there are some for whom it definitely has not. They want to meet, stare you in the eyeballs, and ask you questions about your company (nope, they haven't been to your About Us section!).

◌ **Sales tip:** Trust is very important to the Luddite. Don't feel the need to pressure them, because they will run a mile. Be patient, clever and transparent.

The Geek Buyer

◌ **Personality:** Detail, detail, detail! Analytical by nature, this person has just done a Master's Degree on you! They know more about your company, product and your team than you do. So be prepared.

◌ **They say:** "Give me evidence!"

◌ **Selling to a Geek:** Know your world, and theirs, as best you can. Miss a statistic, or make up a number, and you will get found out. Did we tell you to be prepared?!

⊃ **Sales tip:** Recognise their genius. Be natural, authentic and believable. Let them know that they are in experienced hands.

Summary

- Walk a mile in your customer's shoes by asking our 14 key questions.
- Customers want quick, accurate advice.
- Customers may have to involve more decision makers due to the tight economy.
- Customers have a six-stage buying cycle; however, they might not be on your radar until stage 4.
- Know what modern personality your buyers have: Pulse, Bloggy, Luddite, or Geek.

TIME TO EVOLVE! YOUR SALES TOOLKIT:

1.   Download our free Customer Decision Making Cycle Worksheet. Use this in your next sales meeting to determine how you can influence the customer at each part of the cycle.
2.   During our training we explore buyer personalities and preferences. Receive a 20% discount voucher for our Complete Telesales Skills Open Workshop.
3.   Receive a free sales training worksheet on Customer Personality Analysis. Spend two weeks marking which customers appear in which quadrant. That way you can analyse who you spend the majority of your time selling to.

To access the Natural Training sales resource centre for your 29 FREE resources, simply register online at www.naturaltraining.com/bonusresources

Chapter 3 - Crafting a winning value proposition

Q: "What's your pitch?"
A: "We're real cheap."
George Clooney answers Ewan McGregor –
Men Who Stare at Goats

A strong value proposition is the foundation of every sale: it is a powerful backbone that drives each part of the process. You need to understand your value proposition, strengthen it, and articulate it in a way that moves buyers to action. The modern day buyer must clearly see the two dominant forces in the sale - value and results – very early on in your engagement. And let's face it, in today's market you don't get a second chance to make a good first impression. It's simple: read this chapter to make sure your value proposition makes you money.

Value is the most important dynamic in selling today

The topic we get asked most about in our sales training is value selling. This is due mainly to clients being able to source the same product as you have, at a discounted margin. Will the product be the same quality as yours? Maybe, maybe not. The point is, customers will perceive the cheaper product as being the same quality as your product - unless you build value into your own product. That's absolutely one of your key roles in sales – to build great value.

43

"Cheaper is the last refuge of the marketer unable to invent a better product and tell a better story." Seth Godin

HERE'S AN EXAMPLE...

At Natural Training, we give free 4Gb flash drives away during our presentation skills training. The flash drive holds a couple of each delegate's presentations on video, plus some extra training resources.

Recently, we went out to the UK market for flash drives with our logo. We had a strict budget of £3.50 per unit. The closest we could find to that price was £5.20, and even then it would have involved buying far more flash drives than we wanted. This was after weeks of talking to suppliers and trying to get some pricing and quality assurance.

So, as none of the flash drives were made in the UK, we found out the name of a Chinese manufacturer who supplied the companies we were dealing with. Rightly or wrongly, we perceived that the UK companies were acting as intermediaries anyway, simply marking up the product that they were sent from the manufacturer. We placed an order with the Chinese manufacturer and our flash drives, complete with logo, were delivered three weeks later at £2.50 per unit.

There are two points to this story:

1. We perceived that we were buying 'things' – simple commoditised products that had little value beyond their function. No supplier had changed our minds about this.
2. Despite us dealing extensively with six UK-based flash drive providers, not one of them was able to

build sufficient added value into the sale. Even though we asked repeatedly, we received no discount, no quality assurance or guarantee and nothing else that added value such as offers to speak to satisfied customers. We did not feel any love or value from the relationships that had developed – most were transactional price quotes from hungry, demanding salespeople, displaying little personality, care or advice beyond the immediate requirement.

This situation might be happening to you right now. If you don't build value into the sale, then you probably won't get the business. That's why we need strong value propositions that differentiate what we do and protect us from situations where our customers walk into the arms of grateful, cheaper suppliers.

So, what is a value proposition?

A value proposition is the attention grabber of your sales efforts. Consider this: what is it that grabs your attention as you walk past a news stand in the morning? That's right, the headline!

We all like to think that the fun part of journalism is writing headlines, coming up with catchy one-liners that sell the content of the story in one digestible line. It's actually pretty tough, especially under pressure when the paper is going to print!

In traditional selling, you were the news story and the headline was your value proposition. (Let's face it: most are seller-centric.) In modern day selling, your customer is the news story and the headline they will read is your customer-centric value proposition. Your value proposition is, therefore, a clear message of what you provide to your customers and will be used early on in your sale – sometimes within seconds! This is what should be visible on your company website, business card and any sales and marketing collateral.

If a prospect asks you what you do or what you sell, it's your value proposition that will clearly explain this to them. So let's see what your current value proposition is.

In the following box, please answer the following question: What do you sell?

Chances are your answer to the question talks about your company and product or service. Is this value proposition therefore all about you?

Insider Tip: This is one of the biggest mistakes salespeople make when crafting their value proposition.

Let's re-engineer that question. What do your customers actually **buy** from you? This time focus on them:

This time round, you are starting to talk about the value and results that customers receive when using your product or service.

Much better, because it relates to your customer, not to you.

Today's prospects and customers don't want to hear what you do! They want to hear about the value and the results they will gain from using your product or service. To gain and maintain attention, and then convert those prospective customers, you need to start selling what your customers actually want to buy:

1. Value
2. Results

YOU ARTICULATE THE VALUE AND RESULTS BY CRAFTING A WINNING VALUE PROPOSITION.

Crafting a winning value proposition should be easy to do. After all, you work within your company, you know your product or service inside out, and you talk to customers every day of the week. However, during our sales training workshops we often find that sales professionals like you find this process quite difficult. Why? Because you get so involved with your own product or service. And when you are close to something, it's difficult to see it clearly.

Salespeople very rarely take stock and actually think about the real value and results that customers get from using their solutions. This makes a value proposition incredibly hard to craft.

Key Question: If you find it difficult to articulate your value proposition clearly, how difficult do you think it is for your prospects and customers to see it?

Seller-focused or weak value propositions certainly won't crack it with today's modern day buyer. Therefore, in this chapter we are going to help you to craft a winning value proposition.

HERE'S AN EXAMPLE OF A WEAKER VALUE PROPOSITION...

"Our company name is ShinyWeb and we specialise in providing website design services. We have been rated as one of the best design companies in the UK."

This is a weak value proposition because it doesn't clearly state who you work with. It is seller-focused and talks all about you rather than the value and results customers get from your services. This is the subtle difference that can transform sales results!

Also, if you're going to use a statement with a word such as 'rated' or 'awarded', you must back it up with some evidence. Don't forget that at least half the buyers you will encounter need proof that you can do what you say you can do. (See the previous chapter for details of modern buyer behaviour.) If you're using a weak value proposition like that, it's quite simple; today's time conscious decision makers may not be engaged in the sale, meaning you are fighting a losing battle from the start.

The FIVE key elements to value proposition creation

So, what makes a great value proposition? It's actually pretty simple when you break it down into five key areas as we have done. The first three areas are essential, and the last two turn a good proposition into a great one. (See Fig 3.1)

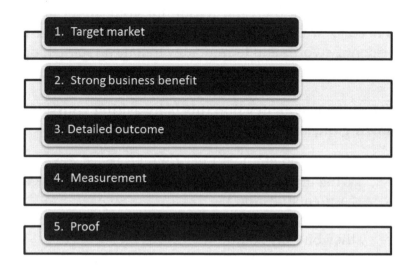

1. Target market

2. Strong business benefit

3. Detailed outcome

4. Measurement

5. Proof

Fig 3.1: The 5 key elements of a value proposition

1) Who is your target market?

Identifying your target market is an important first step. Customers like to know you work within their industry and understand it. If you have multiple target markets, you should have multiple value propositions for each one as the value, results and personal or business benefit they gain from your product or service may be different.

2) A valid business benefit

Customers don't buy products or services unless there is a business benefit - especially in today's market. As an example, very few of us buy or upgrade to the latest phone simply because they have just launched into the marketplace. Instead, we buy on a strong benefit – such as desiring a better method of communication with our friends or customers. Ease of communication and access to the latest applications make our lives easier. This is the valid reason for buying or upgrading.

When identifying the valid reason for your target market, you need to 'walk a mile in your customer's shoes'. The key is to identify words and terminology that mean something to them. Benefits mean different things to different people.

An effective way to develop this is by asking yourself the following questions:

- What problem does my product/service solve?
- What are the consequences of it not being solved? (A great question!)
- What real business or personal needs will be met if they buy my solution?
- Who will benefit the most and what will the ripple effect be?

After answering these questions, pick out the words that would mean the most to your target market.

For example, corporate decision makers respond well to words such as:

- ✓ Cost
- ✓ Revenue
- ✓ Market share
- ✓ Retention
- ✓ New business
- ✓ Time
- ✓ Profitability
- ✓ Efficiency

Corporate decision makers want to hear these words because it's how they measure success. So, use them!

3) Desired outcome

Using words that mean something to your customers will grab their attention, but it's the desired outcome that will actually keep their attention. Every customer with a valid reason to buy isn't going to buy unless they see results from their purchase. So, the next step is to look at the desired outcome that your customers want and need.

We all want an outcome – don't we? When you buy a product, you ultimately want the goal – or better still you want the goal, and the extra benefit! Or what Seth Godin calls the "free prize". For example, to stay at the Beach Rotana Hotel in Abu Dhabi is to guarantee a wonderful night's sleep (benefit). The free prize is the service you receive from the wonderful staff.

Using the same example of a corporate decision maker, this would mean words such as:

- ✓ Increased
- ✓ Decreased
- ✓ Improvement
- ✓ Faster
- ✓ Reduced
- ✓ Minimised
- ✓ Additional

BRINGING THE FIRST THREE ELEMENTS TOGETHER

It's only when you join (1) target market, (2) valid business reason for buying, and (3) desired outcome together that you have the three essential elements of your value proposition. You'll have covered the two features of the sale that today's customers are interested in: value and results. While the first three elements are essential, the final two are beautiful add-ons.

HERE ARE THE FINAL TWO...

4) Measurement
You can strengthen your value proposition even more by bolting on measurements that appeal to prospective customers. Measurable results truly appeal to the modern day buyer and will differentiate you from your competitors. The more specific you can be with your measurements, the stronger your value proposition will be.

For example:

- ✓ 400% increase
- ✓ 20% cost reduction
- ✓ Three times faster

5) Proof
We are now onto the final stages of crafting a winning value proposition. It's time to back up your statement with some evidence and proof. By proof, we mean weaving in a credible customer experience or story to back up the measurements you have used.

HERE'S A GREAT EXAMPLE...

We recently worked with EMC technologies on a sales training programme to help 200 salespeople to pick up the phone and prospect to customers. As a direct result of implementing the new strategies and techniques we taught them, they increased their overall sales revenue by 400%, giving them an audited 20:1 ROI. As a result, we won a National Training Award in 2010.

It's simple; including measurements and proof will make you money because customers will sit up and take notice.

And the easiest way to obtain information on measurable results is to create a sales toolkit of case studies and testimonials. To do this, begin with your current database of customers, asking "Who are our biggest supporters?"

Remember to create testimonials that include some form of measurable result if possible. If you don't have this type of information, then it's simply a case of speaking with your existing clients to see which ones would be happy to provide you with some numbers that indicate real business benefits – profit, ROI, revenue etc.

Create and test that value proposition

Now you need to create and test your proposition ensuring you include as many of the FIVE elements as you can. To help you, we have included an easy to use Value Proposition Creator, which you will find in the Natural Training Sales Resource Centre (full details are available at the end of this chapter).

HERE IS AN EXAMPLE OF A WINNING VALUE PROPOSITION TO GET YOU STARTED...

"We are a specialist SEO company that helps customers within the financial industry to turn their websites into revenue generators, quickly. In fact, we recently helped one of your competitors to increase their website conversion rate by 150%. In year one alone, for every dollar they spent with us, they received $500 back."

Note how the value proposition is unique. This is a fundamental point. Matt Groening said once that good characters should be recognisable in silhouette, which The Simpsons certainly are! Likewise, your value proposition should be so unique that you could cover up your company name and it still apparent that it's yours, and doesn't belong to any of your competitors.

To summarise, **strong value propositions open doors and create opportunities for you to sell.** Taking the time out to clarify your value proposition is time well spent for the modern day sales professional and is highly recommended.

Insider Tip: Use your value proposition within your introduction to sales calls, sales messaging, and when communicating with prospective clients. When you get to the chapter 'How to use LinkedIn as a lead generation tool', you can also use your value proposition there.

TIME TO EVOLVE! YOUR SALES TOOLKIT:

1. Read our free article – 'Value Selling Warren Buffet style'. Start speaking value to
    clients just like Buffett: "Price is what you pay. Value is what you get."
2. Use the Natural Training Value Proposition Creator to develop your ultimate value
    proposition. Try it with five clients and refine it until it's perfect.

Summary

- The most important dynamic in selling today is value – become an expert in it!
- If you don't build value, you won't get the sale.
- In light of today's competitive market, it's important to have a strong, punchy and high-impact value statement.

- Your value proposition is central to your sales efforts in today's selling evolution.
- Value and results are the key features of a value proposition.
- Value creation relies on five key factors: target market, benefit, outcome, measurement and proof.
- The Value Proposition Generator will help you to build the ultimate statement of value.

To access the Natural Training sales resource centre for your 29 FREE resources, simply register online at www.naturaltraining.com/bonusresources

Chapter 4 - Getting through to decision makers

"Nothing is more responsible for the good old days than a bad memory."
Franklin Pierce Adams

Is sales the most demanding profession in the world? You might be the best negotiator, proposal writer or closer in the company, but all of these count for little without a strategy to reach the right decision making person or team. Selling has evolved from simply getting past gatekeepers, or charming a PA. While these skills are still handy, decision makers are harder to reach for a variety of new reasons, which we will explore in this chapter. We will also identify the most effective strategies to help.

Recently we saw an interesting comment on a pre-workshop questionnaire from a delegate at one of our advanced sales training workshops. Here it is, word for word:

"Looking right now at my pipeline, I think I could close 70% of it and make £10,000 in personal income this month, if only I could talk to the decision maker. As it stands, my day is spent talking to everyone else except for the person who can really help me. They are simply not able, or don't want to, take my call, leaving a trail of reasons, excuses and bullshit around them that is really getting me down. Any help appreciated."

This isn't just happening to one salesperson - it's happening everywhere. We hear it from salespeople all the time. It's not that customers aren't saying "yes" – it's just that they are saying nothing. They are not able to be contacted, unavailable and, in some cases, unaccountable.

They have their defences set up to avoid taking calls from anyone who is not a close colleague, a large customer, their mother or the Prime Minister.

As a result, pipelines are overly inflated with status comments such as "tried again, no response" next to them; Sales Managers are getting frustrated and salespeople are considering other professions. If you recognise these problems, and you need to move your client out of your pipeline and into your bottom line, then this chapter is for you.

Begin with the person, not the problem!

As always at Natural Training, we start first with the decision maker, to map out what is actually happening in their world.

HERE IS WHAT WE KNOW ABOUT DECISION MAKERS TODAY:

1. **They are potentially being bombarded with sales approaches.**

One of our clients, an HR Director from a large company, said she gets 20 individual approaches. "A week?" we asked. "A day," she replied, rolling her eyes. "I'm frightened to turn my email on any more or to listen to my voicemail. I must be on a marketing list somewhere." That's not to say we should give up. Far from it. In fact, the same HR Director went on to say: "Despite having what I consider great defences set up, a couple of calls a day still get through. I don't know how they do it, but they do." So, that's 10% of callers getting through. Therefore we need to reframe the question from "Can you get through?" to "What can I do to be in the 10% who do get through?"

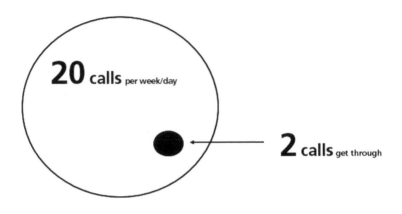

Fig 4.1: Decision maker breakthroughs: Even the decision makers with the best defences talk to 10% of callers

2. Decision makers are being urged to spend money more wisely

This has created an unprecedented level of nervousness with spending. 'Fat cat' banking salaries and excessive government spending have been getting lots of media, and this means that shareholders and company owners have been telling their staff to get more competitive quotes, be more vigilant with costs and economise where possible.

3. Defences are better set up

Customers are now wise to the tactics of cold callers, and

gatekeepers are more educated than ever. The traditional role of gatekeepers being PAs and receptionists has continued, but the gatekeeper role has evolved to include colleagues and technology (using 'out of office' notices, for example.).

4. Quality competitors

There has always been competition. But today's natural sales evolution features more educated, quality competition. For example, the emails and phone call approaches, plus the websites, of companies originating in India and China are now significantly improved. This means your average decision maker has more choice, and a variety of interesting approaches at appealing prices – not just a few local choices.

5. Mobile working habits

At Natural Training, we have 18 full-time equivalent staff, from temp IT and Finance through to Trainers, Sales and Directors. Yet our office will only ever have four to six people in it at any one time. In fact, we have never got together in one room as a company, and probably never will. (Although we do try!) Is this unusual? Not at all – it is the way the world is trending. Research from Cisco found that three out of five workers say that they don't need to be in the office, and only 46% feel that they are more productive when they do go into the office. Large companies like Dell say that over one third of their workforce will be mobile by 2014.

6. The age of search

Google has changed the buying rules. Ten years ago, well-organised customers were still keeping a file of information on your services that they might use one day. Now, there is less need. With Google enjoying significant market dominance, (upwards of 90% of online buying searches are starting with it) the decision maker's mindset has changed:

There is less need to hear about what you do now, because I can search for what I want, when I want.

7. Preferred supplier lists (PSL)

Decision makers are told by their executive chain what they can and cannot buy. Many larger companies will have a preferred supplier list on their intranet that they must choose from. While there is no published research on the frequency of companies having and utilising PSLs, our evidence shows that it is around 30% of companies. Moreover, there is a strong bias of PSLs being used within companies with more than 1000 employees. Note: the numbers are inflated even more by companies using the PSL as an excuse to get you off the phone, rather than actually having one in place!

8. Maybe you're just not that convincing

At Natural Training, we love salespeople who shoulder the blame for a sale. Some don't – they tend to blame the customer! But maybe it's not the customer's fault; maybe it really is the salesperson's fault. Maybe the salesperson's communication simply hasn't been persuasive enough to jolt people out of their apathy.

Consider this from Seth Godin:

"I will buy this treat or I will buy nothing, because I don't really need anything. I will buy your consulting services, or I'll continue doing what I'm doing now on that front, which is nothing. I will vote for you or I'll do

61

what I usually do, which is not vote. I'll hire you, or I'll hire no one. While you think your competition is that woman across town, it's probably apathy, sitting still, ignoring the problem... nothing. Stop worrying so much about comparing yourself to every other possible competitor you can imagine and start comparing yourself to nothing. Are you really worth the hassle, the risk, the time, the money? Or can't the prospect just wait until tomorrow?"
http://www.sethgodin.typepad.com

You need to be persuasive, clear and memorable if decision makers are going to give you the time of day. As Seth says, maybe it's apathy that is your main competitor. Maybe your customer just isn't that into you right now. These eight points all relate to what is happening in the mind of your customer. The bottom line is that you have to evolve! If you can catch the decision maker at their desk (now it's only 30% of the time and dropping), then you better make the most of the time you have to communicate with them!

GATEKEEPERS STILL TEND TO BE THE BIGGEST ISSUE

Despite the way decision makers have evolved, the biggest issue coming from our training delegates is still gatekeepers rejecting their phone call approaches. Here are a few phrases that you may know very well:

- ➲ "We have a no name policy."
- ➲ "Sorry he doesn't take cold calls."
- ➲ "Have you spoken to her before?"
- ➲ "Can you please send an email to goesnowhere@panasonic.com?"

➲ "We're fine right now, thank you."(Without knowing what it is you do!)
➲ "We're happy with our current supplier" or "We have a preferred supplier list."

Insider Tip: It is becoming more commonplace for a customer to have a fake phone number and voicemail box where receptionists can divert cold callers.

Who are gatekeepers?

A gatekeeper has a brief to prevent cold calls from salespeople. This process, also known as 'credentialing', is now used to screen out not only cold callers but also colleagues. At our office in London, we receive around five cold calls per day. Each one of our salespeople will act as gatekeepers for each other and for the Directors.

In some respects, you have to feel for the gatekeeper. They are inundated with sales calls on a daily basis from sales professionals who will say just about anything to try to get a few minutes to showcase their worth in front of the right person.

Without a gatekeeper screening the phone calls and filtering emails, the people at the top would probably be interrupted quite often throughout their day. Some will have their phones on constant voicemail these days simply because of the level of sales calls they receive.

Herein lies the challenge. This is part of sales, and the fact is, as sales professionals you need to think about how you deal with this particular (and significant) barrier to a sale.

In fact, you probably need to spend more time dedicated to it than you might think. If you could talk to decision makers twice as much as you are now, then it follows that you will probably be closing twice the amount of business (all other things being equal). It's a significant issue that is costing you money.

Remember, it is the job of the gatekeeper to channel the right information through to their bosses – your target. If you have a valid reason to be calling and present yourself in the right way then you stand a good chance of getting through.

It helps to have an idea of who you're dealing with.

Categorising gatekeepers will allow you to tailor your approach and apply a bit of strategy to warming up those cold calls.

OUR RESEARCH SHOWS THERE ARE BROADLY THREE TYPES OF GATEKEEPER:

Gatekeeper 1: Those who put you through straight away. Today, these represent no more than 10% of gatekeepers.
Gatekeeper 2: Those who really push you and explore why you're calling and what you need (about 80% fall into this category).
Gatekeeper 3: The fire-breathing dragons who never let anyone through (luckily this only makes up about 10% of gatekeepers). It's important that you recognise which ones you tend to come across. This will help you to develop suitable strategies.

SO, WHAT'S YOUR PLAN TO GET THROUGH TO DECISION MAKERS?

The first thing to do is to examine the mindset you take onto each call – particularly if you find yourself blaming 'them' for not putting you through. So, shift the reason for success from them to you!

Now that you are taking responsibility for your success, you need to think about how you sound and the first few words you use when you speak to a gatekeeper.

Here are the traps you might be falling into:

1. You sound uncertain or nervous.
2. You sound too 'canned' or 'salesy', as if you are reading from a script.
3. You sound unfamiliar. Gatekeepers tend to take the same sorts of calls all the time from the same sorts of people – staff, customers, and regular suppliers. Sound strange, and you will be considered strange!

If any of these three points feature in your calling technique, it should come as no surprise that gatekeepers turn you away every time you call. How do you tell? Simple – record your calls.

Insider Tip: If you don't have access to a recording system, such as Natural Training's Call Doctor, simply call your mobile and leave a message for yourself. Try some variations. Listen to your messages the following day imagining that you are the gatekeeper. Would you let yourself through? Alternatively, do a role play with a colleague or put it on the agenda for your next sales meeting. Spending 10 minutes every day warming up and thinking of new ideas will pay immediate dividends.

WHAT DOES YOUR SALES CALL SAY ABOUT YOU?

Consider this standard introduction to a call: "Hello, my

name's Terry Holmes and I'm calling from Indigo IT. Can I please speak to the person in charge of your IT infrastructure?"

In this call the words are saying one thing. But the real message to the gatekeeper is: "This is a generic sales call – reject!" Alarm bells are sounding in the gatekeeper's head.

If you get a hostile initial response, there's a good chance you'll face an uphill battle from the start. If, however, you begin the call with confidence - avoiding arrogance - then you stand a far greater chance of being put through to the right person.

WHAT DOES THE GATEKEEPER REALLY NEED TO KNOW?

Gatekeepers may ask a variety of questions. But the three questions they will almost always have are:

1. What is your name?
2. What company are you calling from?
3. What is the purpose of your call?

Do you want these questions? NO! Your job isn't to engage in a discussion with a gatekeeper. You want to talk to decision makers. In fact, the longer you take talking to gatekeepers, the more chance you have of showing a crack in the armour, so this is a discussion that should be kept as brief as possible.

What's the best strategy to ensure that you don't have to answer any of those questions? Simple - answer them all in your opening line so the gatekeeper has nothing left to ask!

Your opening line, or message, must be brief, purposeful and it must answer all of the questions that would normally be used to filter you out. Your name and company name are easy. It's the third part salespeople struggle with – the purpose of the call. This is where you can lose the call. You have to know exactly why you're calling and be convinced that your time is just as important as that of those you are calling. (Your tone in particular can make you sound unsure – you have to sound natural!) You have something of value to give to your decision maker, and this is the mindset you must take into the call.

Here's a sample of a very straightforward opening line – note the relaxed, natural language:

- ⊃ "Morning – Matt from Kaiser Physio – is Bill there, please? It's about his back appointment."
- ⊃ "Afternoon – John from Logitech – Kelly Bronk please. She will know what the call is regarding."
- ⊃ "Hi Joan, it's Terry from iPrint – Sandra Tully please. She knows why I'm calling."

USE VALUE IN YOUR CALL PURPOSE

Value works. If gatekeepers sense you are of value, or have something of value to give to the prospect, then they will of course be more likely to put you through. The thing about value is that it should be 100% customer-focused, and it needs to be compelling. It needs to be the kind of offer that elicits a 'Yes' response.

Your introduction needs to be focused on the client's problems and priorities. Make it in their interest to forward the call.

Bring value to the call, with:

- ✓ A customer-centric introduction
- ✓ Evidence that you have done research
- ✓ Demonstrations of results
- ✓ Trigger events and relevant 'hooks'
- ✓ The ability to put fear into the heart of the gatekeeper if they don't take action.

AN EXAMPLE IS WEB SECURITY:

- ✓ "Hi Paul, I've done some research into your company, and I believe I've uncovered a potentially serious security flaw in the infrastructure within your firewall simply by breaking in. I need to explain this to your IT Manager so could you put me through please?"

HERE ARE ANOTHER TWO VALUABLE EXAMPLES:

- ✓ "Hi Jill. I have five new Thomas Pink business shirts to be delivered to your Sales Managers as incentives for your sales team. Can I get through to speak about delivery please?"

- ✓ "Morning Rhona – confirming the attendance of Ron and James from Marketing to an evening with Jon Steel – have you got access to their diaries?"

Value via research

If some of those don't yet work for you, then try to demonstrate value via research and good old hard work.

HERE'S AN EXAMPLE...

"Good morning Paul. I've been doing some research on your company over the past couple of months and I can see that you're focusing on breaking into the Indian market. We've consulted with other companies in your industry, like Billabong and Helly Hansen, to generate results including a 37% initial market awareness. We think the head of Marketing would be interested in seeing this, but what do you think, Paul?"

Insider Tip: 'No name' policy? Use other ways to get hold of clients. LinkedIn, for example, is a great resource for getting names of people who work in various roles. Send them a mail, or 'connect' to them. (See Chapter 12 on LinkedIn for more.)

Alarm bells!

The danger of becoming too creative with your route past the gatekeeper is that you fall foul of the golden rules of sales.

These include:

1. Language. You must avoid over-exaggeration of products.
2. Lies. Do not try to lie or manipulate the gatekeeper. They have the power in the relationship, so don't upset them.
3. Quiet confidence. Avoid arrogance, it's off-putting and will only create more of a barrier between you and your target.

Practise and rehearse: What you are going to say if the gatekeeper questions you further?

Some of the questions you must be prepared to answer are:

- "Is this a sales call?"
- "What do you want? Is she/he expecting your call?"
- "Are you on our preferred supplier list?"
- "Are you aware of our 'no names' policy?"
- "Can you just send an email?"

In sales, you must be able to provide confident and assured answers to all of these questions. If you can't, you are not prepared.

Insider Tip: Gatekeepers have a mission to keep you away! Most people give up, but you have nothing to lose. Professionally challenge them by trying a question such as: "What do you suggest I do?"

WHY NOT TRY IT RIGHT NOW?

How would you respond to each of the following questions?

- "Is this a sales call?"
- "Is he/she expecting your call?"
- "Can you just send an email?"
- "Are you aware of our 'no names' policy?"
- "Are you on our preferred supplier list?"

Here are a few answers for you to try:

Question	Answer
"Is this a sales call?"	"Shelley, I have nothing to sell Bob – I have to speak to him this morning. Can I be put through, please?"
"Is he/she expecting your call?"	"Bob knows about us, yes."
"Can you just send an email?"	"Peter, John will be glad you have put me through – can you do so please? Let John know it is Barry Stephens calling."

70

"Are you aware of our 'no names' policy?"	"Yes – but I was used to dealing with Pam, and the role has changed recently."
"Are you on our preferred supplier list?"	"I assume so Greg – I'm new to your account. You are used to dealing with Steve, I think."

DEALING WITH VOICEMAIL

Voicemail is a current defence mechanism. Some of the busier decision makers you are targeting will get 20 voicemails a day and will whiz through them very quickly with their finger poised on the delete function. So it's important to keep it brief, and get most of it out in 10 seconds or less. Avoid typical voicemails, such as:

"Matt, it's Trish from OfficePlants, and we have a special this month on two-for-one plants for your office. I'm in your area tomorrow afternoon – I was wondering whether I could drop over and say hello and show you some of our more exciting options. Please give me a call back on 0423 3432 456..."

Delete! Delete! Delete! The only way this would ever work is if the person was sitting thinking about plants for their office, right then. Is that a 1/1,000 chance? 1/50,000?

There is nothing in this voicemail that would compel a prospect to call you back, which of course is the aim of voicemail. It's not to advertise your services, or tell a story. In sales, voicemail is designed to get a call back.

Getting a call back is a challenge, but not impossible!

Just as 10% of people get through gatekeepers, about 10% of

voicemails get call backs. The trick is to make sure your voicemail is one of the 10% that do receive a call back.

The key is to stimulate desire, curiosity and a willingness to ACT.

How about these:

1. "Hi Peter. It's Bill here. Call me back on 0123 456 7891 - that's 0123 456 7891."
2. "Hi Kelly – Tracey from Marketing passed your name on to me. Can you call me this morning on 0123 456 7891?"
3. "Graham, Paul. I'm told that you are the only person at Triage who can answer my question. Can you call me back please on 0123 456 7891?"
4. "Hi Gunther, it's Lisa here. Your name came up in a meeting this morning. Call me back on 0123 456 7891 - that's 0123 456 7891."

In these examples, we are delivering a relevant and intriguing voicemail that takes less than ten seconds. They have been tested by Natural Training to deliver up to 10 times as many call backs – choose the one or two that you are comfortable using, and let us know your results!

FINAL TIPS ON GATEKEEPERS – AVOID THEM ALTOGETHER!

If you know your way around a modern phone system, then you may be able to avoid gatekeepers altogether.

Here are our top tips:

- Change the last three digits on the phone number. The call will probably go through to an extension that is not Reception. Simply ask whoever picks up

to put you through to the department you are after.
- When in a voicemail, you can press 'zero' and go back to switch and keep on asking for different people. Don't rest until you speak to someone!
- Great salespeople build a picture of an organisation. Even if you speak to someone from Finance, and you want Marketing, you can still ask them some questions about who's who in Marketing, any recent initiatives or even budgets. Keep building that picture!
- If you keep coming up against a vigilant gatekeeper who won't put you through even though you feel the customer definitely wants to talk to you, then ask someone else from your organisation to call the gatekeeper and keep them busy for a few minutes on the phone. While they are busy, simply place the call to the person you are after.
- Try calling out of hours – say from 7am in the morning, and from 6pm at night. You will be pleasantly surprised at who picks up the phone out of hours!

More top tips for getting through to decision makers:

In sales, you only really have one true enemy and that is silence. Anything is better than silence. You can work with everything else – objections, conditions, people messing you about, "no", "yes", "maybe" and everything in between. But silence gives you nothing to work with except insecurity, fear and wonder. So, even if you aren't getting a "yes", keeping powerful decision makers engaged and alert to you is enough for now. Think of some ways to add value to their lives, and know when to stop selling, and start enriching. Americans use a term called an 'abundance mentality' quite often – it's a good one for you to adopt with your most important decision makers. Keep giving value, and watch what comes back to you!

Email is another great weapon for getting through. Avoid overly long emails – try to get your whole message into the first one or two lines, just as you would the purpose of your call. Attach anything that will otherwise clutter up your email. Focus on your subject line – if it is interesting enough, people will open it, or read the first couple of lines in the auto-previewer. A couple of tricks:

- ✓ Try putting RE: in front of your message. This makes it seem like a response rather than an introduction.
- ✓ Put a common name or theme in the message: RE: Pamela Dawson (if Pamela works there or is an industry-recognised name).

In your email body, you need to start with a strong purpose, as you would with a call or meeting. Make a personal observation – start with "I noticed something recently, John…" This shows you are current, and ought to set you apart from the pack.

Using the same type of voicemail and email message each time just doesn't cut it in today's evolved selling world. For example, "Have you read our proposal yet?" isn't really going to provide a circuit-breaker for their current lack of response. Decision makers will avoid you if they think that you are just going to ask them the same question time after time, so hit them with a fresh angle. Think "How can I add value to them?" rather than "How can I get a sale?" and you will be part of the way there.

74

Try Skype. A call or an instant message on Skype is a point of difference that might help. You can easily do a search on their first and last name. And don't worry if it appears that they are offline – send the message anyway; they will get it.

Tweeting can be a great way to influence your decision makers. Keep them coming, and they will get noticed!

Outlook can be used effectively – particularly appointment setting. It will appear in your decision maker's diary for them to reject or confirm, which is a nice engagement strategy. You can put an agenda in the body of the appointment, and attach information as required.

LinkedIn is another way to break through to decision makers. (We touched on it in this chapter, but Chapter 12 explores it in more detail. You should read it because it will help you get through to decision makers.)

Try a knowledge gift. Give them something that will enrich their work life – it could be a PDF of a report from the 'Harvard Business Review' or a link to a news item, for example.

Invite them to an event. There are always industry events in the calendar. Most decision makers like to keep up-to-date and have a free glass of nice wine.

Have the courage to find them when they are not at their desk. In the past, when people weren't at their desk, you were perhaps more hesitant to call because they were off work or travelling. Now, they are just as likely to be on the road working, so they might not mind a call as much. Recently, we called a prospective customer who was more than willing to talk because he was standing at a long check-in queue at an airport. He had absolutely nothing else to do! If you know that they are staying in a particular hotel or at a conference, and don't have their mobile, try them at the venue or try making contact via a colleague.

Put a strategy into place for covering the other important people in the organisation. Yes, there might only be one true decision maker, but you still have work to do to sell to other important customers in that organisation. At Natural Training, we have a system called BITE, which stands for Buyer, Influencer, Technical Assessor and End-user. The idea is to get around to each of the four people, not just the main one, because it's likely that all will be deciding whether to use your services. (See our Sales Toolkit at the end of this chapter for more help on BITE.)

Never, ever give up. It might take six times as many attempts to get through to an important decision maker today, but that's okay. Stay confident and don't listen to the voice inside your head saying, "They don't want to speak to me". They're just busy. So keep it varied and creative, try at different times, and put a strategy in place to deal with it. Be bold – **they won't call the sales police!**

As always, the knowledge of new ideas and strategies does not equal application.Only application equals application! There are loads of ideas in this chapter, some of which you will like, and some of which will not be for you. The only way to know whether they work is to try them in your environment. That's what adaptation and evolution is all about! There is no replacement for hard work and on-the-job application - you can't beat jumping in at the deep end!

Even a 1% improvement can change your world!

Steve Jobs' father made cabinets for a living. He used to teach Steve about quality and how even the tiniest sacrifice wasn't to be tolerated. For example, no-one sees the back of a cabinet, so you could in theory use cheap wood. "However, while the customer wouldn't know that it was cheap, you would" he would tell Steve, "and that's not good enough." Steve Jobs took this philosophy right throughout his career at Apple – making tiny, 1% improvements wherever he could – for example a higher quality of glass for i-phone that he specifically sourced from Dow Corning. There was no urgent need to find something better – the current standard of glass was considered fine by other phone manufacturers and consumers seemed okay with it. However that one bit of insistence from Jobs resulted in the creation of Gorilla Glass – now the scratch and damage-proof standard in mobile devices around the world. The accumulation of 1% improvements by Jobs resulted in world-class product lines and great differentiation from competitors. It also meant Jobs could sleep at night soundly.

Today, selling is a bit like this scenario. Sometimes it is difficult to make any big changes, because you are doing everything pretty well already. That's why it's good to realise that the real improvements can be in the small changes. It's a word or two to gatekeepers, or a Tweet, or a subtle email subject line change that can make all the difference. Selling today is testing, it's playing, and giving things a go. Selling is working around the boundaries of normality to find a point of difference that will give you an edge. And these edges do pay off. For example if you make 1000 approaches a month, even a 1% improvement on your ability to get through to decision makers is an extra 10 conversations that can result in a big sale. And these types of ideas have worked in the past for the customers of Natural Training at a much higher efficacy rate than 1%.

The latest evolution of sales isn't 'scramble around frantically trying to sell'. Instead, it's working out what great value means to your target list, planning when and how to contact them, and calmly executing that plan. Lots of salespeople are still making great money. Be a part of that group by working out how to speak to more decision makers, more often.

Summary

- Getting through to decision makers is one of the biggest issues in sales today.
- There are eight key reasons for your decision maker being busier and more defensive.
- Gatekeepers are preventing you from making money – you need to have a strategy in place to handle them.
- The modern gatekeeper's role has extended to colleagues and managers – not just receptionists.
- Value and variation will both open doors for you.
- If you leave a voicemail message, make it intriguing enough for them to WANT to call you back!
- Have multimedia strategies to utilise, rather than just the traditional phone.

TIME TO EVOLVE! YOUR SALES TOOLKIT:

1. Stream our audio file 'Five tips to handle gatekeepers and leave voicemail'.

2. Send us an audio recording to evolve@naturaltraining.com of you trying out some of these techniques – and our expert coaches will give you some free feedback!

3. Widen and deepen your decision making base by appealing to Buyers, Influencers, Technical Assessors and End-Users. Download our free BITE tool.

4. Selling today is testing and playing around the edges. Try out each approach over the next four weeks, and make it your own with tweaks according to your natural style. Keep a record of which approaches work the best.

5. Bypassing gatekeepers altogether is a great strategy! Use LinkedIn for two weeks as a way of sending messages through to your decision makers. Don't forget to read the chapter about LinkedIn!

To access the Natural Training sales resource centre for your 29 FREE resources, simply register online at www.naturaltraining.com/bonusresources

Chapter 5 - NaturalFlow™ contemporary questioning techniques

"If you know what story your customers live in, you can sell to them with ease."
Perry Marshall

"Seek first to understand, then to be understood," explained the late Stephen Covey in his book, The 7 Habits of Highly Effective People. This is the basis for the chapter, because once you finally get to engage with today's customer, your next step is to ask intelligent questions focused on their needs. If you can get this part right, you can let your questioning do the selling for you...

Let's have a brief look at the way selling has evolved:

One hundred years ago, the most important sales skill was talking, or 'soapboxing'. Salespeople would stand or 'spruik' on a platform or box, and hope that their message stuck.

Fifty years ago, the most important sales skill was persuasion. With personal customer contact such as door-to-door, a few questions would help the salesperson launch into a more tailored, persuasive presentation.

In recent history, various models and techniques such as consultation, facilitation and being a trusted advisor, have changed the face of selling. **Yet throughout all of these evolutionary sales stages, questioning skills have retained their absolute dominance as the most important personal selling skill.** "Get to know your customer's situation, and sell them something tailored to their needs" would be the world's shortest, yet most effective, sales book.

The role of questioning is as important as ever. But what has changed is the way you ask questions.

Selling has evolved in the past five years in a big way. As we have previously mentioned, by the time customers have reached you, it is likely that they have done their homework and have less time to talk. They need you, the Sales Maker, to make it happen for them and will have a different, more urgent mindset to customers in the past.

So the questions you need to ask ought to be intelligent, high-yield (getting a bigger answer return per word) and precise. Customers don't want to repeat themselves, or give you simple information that you could find out elsewhere. If you only have five minutes on a sales call, then you need to have three to five questions ready that really count. And if they are 'big yield' questions then all the better, because they will demand an answer rich in detail from the customer.

Let's say you only have an hour to prepare for a meeting. Which of the following two categories do you fall into?

1. You spend the majority of your time thinking about your products, how to present them and what exactly to say about them. You think about how you will showcase them to the customer in a way that excites them and demonstrates your expertise. You

also conduct some background research on the company, and the person you are meeting.

2. You spend the majority of your time preparing the questions you want to ask, while working out your real value, as well as allocating some time to researching the customer and the company.

The first category is good, but it misses out the most important ingredient: preparing to ask effective questions. The second category works better in today's environment, because customers want to:

✓ Know that you have done your homework (see Chapter 12).
✓ Give you a little bit more about themselves (this chapter).
✓ Understand the value you offer (see Chapter 3).

Questions provide much more than information

In our sales training workshops, we ask delegates a simple question: "What are the advantages of asking questions?" It's an obvious question, which deserves an obvious answer: questions help you find out information. But there are more, perhaps less obvious answers about the benefits of great questioning skills.

QUESTIONS HELP YOU TO:

✓ Develop a BESPOKE solution (bespoke means customised, and customised means higher value).
✓ Find out issues (salespeople sell on issues).
✓ Engage the prospective customer – particularly if they are great questions.

✓   Make people LIKE you – sometimes likeability is the only thing that separates competitors going for a big ticket deal.

✓   Gain credibility! It's difficult to say "I'm smart", although some salespeople will try! If you ask smart, well considered questions, however, chances are your customers will think that you are a person worth doing business with. Smart questions reflect smart people. Don't forget that society rates people with good questioning skills very highly: think of people like Jeremy Paxman in the UK, Chris Matthews in the USA and Andrew Denton in Australia.

ASKING QUESTIONS IS EASY, RIGHT?

Asking questions, just like breathing, is one of the most normal and natural things in the world. Three-year-olds are particularly adept at questioning. From the moment they open their eyes in the morning until the time they close them at night, they question the world around them. That talent, that natural curiosity to understand the world around us, never really leaves us.

As long as you're not afraid to talk, questions tend not to be much of a problem for you. This is why at Natural Training we find that salespeople don't spend much time on them. It's as natural as breathing – an automatic natural response that you don't really have to worry about, right?

Well, wrong. Very wrong. There are questions, and then there are questions that sell. They are two different things.

THIS IS BEST SHOWN BY EXAMPLE:

Question	Questions that Sell
"Could I please speak to the person in charge of HR?"	"Helen, can you please help me get an important message through to Margaret in HR?"
"What is it you do at Steele Inc., Helen?"	"Helen, I noticed online that you are streamlining your consultant workflow. Can I ask you please to donate a few comments for an article I'm writing on how consultants engage with employers?"
"Do you have any IT needs now?"	"John, I saw your comment on LinkedIn about your new office move. Can I ask you please how much progress you have made in sorting out your network architecture, particularly the way your new branch coordinates with head office?"

The questions on the left might have worked five or ten years ago, but will probably not work for you today. The reason is they lack imagination, creativity, focus and credibility. Any salesperson on day one of their job can ask those types of questions. They won't yield a big or interesting answer, because they are ill-considered.

The questions on the right, however, instantly position you as someone worth talking to. Great questions aren't necessarily easy to come up with, which is why not many people come up with them! But if you are to brand yourself as a winner in today's market, this is the attitude you need.

Insider Tip: There is some evidence that questions can stimulate various parts of the brain. Two types of stimulation are brought on by Recitation Questions and Dialogue Questions. The former are questions that recall previous knowledge – in other words, the customer knows the answer, or they have been asked it many times. Dialogue Questions require more deep and complex thought. You might like to ask a question for example that creates a comparison that will lead to change.

Two things you need to know to ask really great questions in TODAY's market:

1. Questions thrive in structure.
2. Questions should be natural not interrogative.

Both of these dynamics are covered in our NaturalFlow™ Questioning System. While this book isn't designed to give you everything you need to know about NaturalFlow™, it will help you to get a really strong overview of how you can apply these techniques.

NaturalFlow™ Questioning System

Structure & Benefits

Questions thrive in structure. While there are many different question structures in the market (recently we saw one with eight stages!), most are difficult to use. They result in a jerky, unnatural delivery as salespeople move from one stage to the next.

Customers today simply won't tolerate salespeople using old style questioning models or using rigid, linear questioning techniques. It makes them feel that the person asking is not listening to their needs, that they are repeating themselves and that the questioner is inflexible in their approach. They certainly don't want to feel the salesperson is asking questions for the sake of it or interrogating them. Interrogations usually result in a nervous, agitated customer who can quite clearly see the questioning process unfolding before them. You feel selfish to them. Instead, questions should help to develop an easy dialogue that helps customers relax into the conversation – the perfect conditions for giving you the information you need to sell.

At Natural Training, we believe in a questioning structure and process that FLOWS – that makes the customer relaxed and more willing to provide the type of information you want. Importantly, customers shouldn't be able to pick up that you are using techniques – it has to be natural.

THE NATURALFLOW™ QUESTIONING STRUCTURE

We designed Natural Flow Questioning to create the perfect environment and question bank for the modern day buyer. This is more than a selling tool – it's a cultural shift. Even better, it is flexible, simple to understand and use. The key to effective questioning is to imagine a funnel. As the funnel draws tighter, so do the questions as they move closer to crystallising the customer's needs.

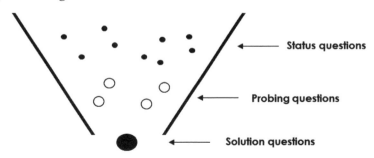

Fig 5.1: NaturalFlow™ questioning funnel

Status questions: Help you to seek to understand the client environment. Status questions are asked without prejudice and will help you to identify what the customer already knows, how much they have already researched and what triggered them to start looking around. Essentially, your status questions should give you an answer to this query: Is this a business priority?

Insider Tip: Remember that your customer may have conducted a large amount of research online before engaging with salespeople. The educated modern day buyer will not tolerate salespeople asking basic sales questions to determine what their needs are. (There is more on status questions later in this chapter.)

Probing questions: These questions seek to develop and prioritise customer issues. In some cases, the client won't know their issues, especially today's busy decision makers, until you have coaxed them out. You need a curious mind and an accurate ear because you might otherwise miss what's really being said. Great salespeople don't miss a thing. They pick up on the clues throughout a conversation and probe the customer for more, more, more! The right types of probes are vital because you can uncover motive, implication and achieve a greater level of emotional tie-in by deploying the right probing questions. (You'll find more on probes later in this chapter.)

Solution questions: These questions help guide the client towards a collaborative rather than prescriptive solution. After some practice, you will be able to encourage the client to articulate how you can help them, not the other way around. (See the detailed section on solution questions.)

Status questions

As the name suggests, we use these questions to try to find out all about the status of a prospective client. What is it like to live a day in their shoes - to really get inside their minds?

These questions take many forms, but here are a few ideas to get you started:

1) High Yield Open Questions: These are like open questions on steroids. Open questions are named that way because they will open up a conversation by opening the mind of the customer. High Yield Open Questions require a big answer – they can't be answered in just one or two words. Instead, they require a more detailed response. (If questions can be answered in one or two words, they are closed questions. Note: closed questions are handy too, so don't believe advice you get about never asking a closed question – all types of questions have a purpose.)

In the old world of selling, you might hear a trainer say, "Open questions start with 'Who', 'What', 'Where', 'When', 'How' and 'Why'." This is nonsense! Questions starting with those words can all be answered in just one, or a few words, meaning that they can all just as easily be closed as open.

For example:

Question: "How are you managing the process of
recruiting kitchen staff?"
Answer: "With great difficulty!"

That didn't help you much, did it? A better way to think is to **increase your yield** from each question.

Here are three ways to begin high-yield questions:

1. "Sally, can you please help me to understand how you are currently managing the process of recruiting kitchen staff…?"
2. "Ahmed, please can you give me three examples of…?"
3. "John, can we make a list together please starting with your biggest priority around…?"

2) Yesterday, Today, Tomorrow Questions: Business is moving along at breakneck speed. And if salespeople are to evolve with it, we need to understand what the buying patterns of our customers have been, are and will be.

That is why we need 'yesterday, today and tomorrow' questions. The benefit of these types of status questions is that it lends questioning a useful sequence, adding depth and time-related context. This enables you to get an accurate snapshot of your client more quickly.

Yesterday questions: Without knowing about a client's past buying patterns, it is difficult to predict what they will do in the future. That's where yesterday questions come in.

Examples:

-   "Barry, can you please help me get a hold of how you have been able to sort this out in the past?"
-   "What have you done in the past to solve your catering needs?"
-   "How have you traditionally gone about archiving your documents?"
-   "When was the first time office temps came on to your radar?"

Today questions: These include questions to ascertain current thought patterns and the status of what is happening NOW.

Examples:

- "Barry, when you think about this project, what are your priorities RIGHT NOW?"
- "How many servers do you currently have and what is their capacity?"
- "What are your current advertising needs, if you had to list a top three?"
- "If I sat down at one of your computers this morning and turned it on, how long would it take to boot up and why?"

Tomorrow questions: Future planning details are crucial to know – even if it's not information you would like to hear (such as whether they are planning to use a cheaper solution!). Without answers to current plans, you don't know what you are selling against.

Examples:

- "Daphne, looking ahead at all of your options, what is your gut feeling about where this is heading?"
- "What are your most urgent future challenges with archiving information?"
- "What plans are in place with you, John and Stephanie, to provide for the security of your employees?"

3) Trigger questions: With the modern day buyer, one of the first questions we would suggest you ask is a trigger question. The term 'trigger question' comes from psychology and is designed to provoke a response. Think of it as hitting your customer's hot button.

The benefits of the trigger question include:

1. Letting the customer know you have done your research.
2. Positioning yourself as someone to be trusted.

How do you generate trigger questions?
You have to carry out the right level of research before the customer conversation. This could generate a range of questions based on one or more of the following trigger events:

- A recent announcement
- New legislation
- New product launch
- A recent blog post or article you read on their LinkedIn profile
- Information you discovered in the company's annual report
- A shift in industry trends

A great way to start off a trigger question is:

- "Bridget, I noticed that..."

This immediately positions you as someone with a discerning eye; a considered sales professional who has gone out of the way to make an observation.

The key here is to use trigger questions to demonstrate your knowledge and understanding of their world. In return, the customer will give you their precious time because you have demonstrated just how valuable you can be.

For instance, if you're a recruitment consultant and 'sell' candidates into resourcing teams, the trigger event could be a change in employment law. The trigger question could be: "Miles, I noticed that the Government has relaxed the law on dismissals. What sort of knock-on effects will this have on you, your company, your team and your industry?"

What kind of trigger questions could you ask in the next sales meeting you attend? See if you can list FIVE questions off the back of some trigger events in the following table.

Trigger Event	Trigger Questions

Remember, you need to be natural, and make the questions flow – this is the secret to NaturalFlow™. When you are writing your questions, you have to be aware of this and not make them overly complicated or 'overworked'.

PROBING QUESTIONS

As we have discussed, status questions help you to understand your customer's current environment. Along the way, we need to probe to find out their issues, because if you don't know what their issues are, then chances are you won't be able to sell. That is where probing questions come in. They help us to find out issues quicker and with great effect. This is so important right now. As we have talked about previously, we are at a crucial part of the natural selling evolution. We are in the phase of low customer time, short customer patience, and highly competitive markets.

From time to time during your questioning you will "sniff out" little glimpses of issues that you can probe around to find out more. To use an iceberg analogy, status questions are on the surface level – 'what they say' – and probing questions go deeper – 'what they mean'.

Figure 5.2: An iceberg is a great analogy for the benefits of effective questioning

Two great benefits of probing questions:

1. Probing uncovers issues: It's hard to sell effectively without understanding your customer's issues. Issues can create headaches, and headaches create needs, and needs create sales. Sometimes, however, people are not aware they have issues until they are asked a few questions. For example, someone could ask you questions about your health, and in the process, you realise you are in desperate need of a holiday. This is the beautiful consequence of probing questions – you are not telling the customer; they discover it for themselves.

2. Probing grows issues: You have to do more than simply tell a customer what to do. As Brian Tracy said, "Telling isn't selling". And probing isn't telling, it's asking. Done well, great probing questions will enlarge issues in your customer's mind as you draw their attention to a specific area of interest within the conversation.

Probing questions will help grow pain and develop gain, both of which you want.

They have the magical effect of re-prioritising issues in the mind of your customer. They are simply brilliant, and a highly coveted skill for today's evolved sales professional.

OUR TOP SIX PROBING QUESTIONS

These aren't stand-alone questions. They are designed to fit in after your status questions to target the issues of customers that you 'sniff out' during conversations. In today's modern business environment, you have to listen really well to pick up the signals. Note: it's normal and easy to listen to what is familiar. However, today's successful salespeople would be much better served by listening to what is different.

Here are our top six probes:

1. **"How did that make you feel?"** Customers' feelings are important – This probe moves the conversation from the logical part of the brain (where sales people usually reside) to the emotional part, where selling can really thrive.

2. **"Could I please have an example of that?"** Examples bring issues to life in the minds of your customers and help you to grow and prioritise them.

3. **"May I please clarify one of your points?"** Seeking clarification is not only okay to do, it's encouraged. Don't let the opportunity go without clarifying your understanding. You might not be able to have another conversation with the client for weeks or months – make the most of the opportunity now!

4. **"What are the implications of (that issue) on your department/team/time?"** Implications or impact is important in business. Like falling dominoes, one small thing can impact another and so on until there is a whole chain of issues to be resolved.

For example, a Company Director may believe that minimising office cleaning services is a clever cost-cutting measure without realising it will have a detrimental impact on productivity. Careful questioning could help him to realise that a dirty work environment will lower staff morale and therefore engagement (a crucial factor in productivity) as well as increase the likelihood of absenteeism. Further questioning could help him to see how an unclean office will also damage the company's image, particularly in the eyes of visiting clients.

5. "Would I be right in saying that you're really passionate about (that issue)?" This type of reflecting probe is very important, as it shows you listening, and will generate more discussion around a significant issue. It's a nice change from the usual probing questions too.

6. "That's interesting – could I hear more about that please?" A nice, simple probe, but an effective one. Probing isn't rocket science – it's a way for you to find out more selling issues. Simple, but important.

Insider Tip: For the world's simplest probe, try silence. The act of saying NOTHING can work well to get the information you need.

In our sales training courses, we cover the art of probing quite extensively. And yes, it is an art. Our evidence is that only a small percentage of modern sales professionals are using probing questions effectively - yet this one skill can be a big difference in today's evolved sales world featuring smaller, highly important customer interactions.

SOLUTION QUESTIONS

Imagine you are in the middle of a discussion with a customer. Your excellent questioning has uncovered a number of issues, and you have explored them, grown them and helped to re-prioritise them in the mind of the customer. The stage is set for you to do some solving! Not only can you help, but you know EXACTLY what they need, right?

Well that may be right, but you still have to be careful not to jump in prematurely and tell them something that they are either already doing, or have recently solved themselves. That's where solution questions come in. Solution questions are designed to get the customer thinking about the type of solution you have in mind, without telling them. (Remember, telling isn't selling.) Asking questions to help your customers arrive at a solution is a much smarter way to sell, as it helps them to buy in to your solution. It's collaborative, it helps generate ideas, and it's very much a feature of the way customers like to do business today.

It's also about learning more!

The only thing that you really learn when you give a client a solution is whether they like it or not. Yet, if you ask solution questions for a short time beforehand, you can find out so much more to get the solution right.

For example, solution questions give you an insight into their buying patterns, including their habits, and fears about buying. You might find out that they are already significantly advanced with choosing a competitor's solution! Don't be afraid of this information – you need to know it. There is a lot of wasted selling time spent with customers who never have any intention of buying from you. This is all important when it comes to developing your solution, or moving them out of your pipeline and concentrating on customers who do want to do business with you. You may also learn how they interact with colleagues, their time management and how they envisage using your product or service, which allows for a greater emotional connection.

Here are a few solution questions for you to try out – but only when you feel instinctively that you have an

understanding of their issues:

- "Brendan, what does the solution look like to you?"
- "Stacy, what have you tried in the past to overcome any of these issues?"
- "John, are you on a path to solving this, or at least knowing what **not** to do?"
- "Claire, what might be the next steps here, do you think?"

Or you can try some more advanced solution questions with extra muscle added in:

"We recently worked with another client in a similar field to you with practically identical needs. They took our Zenith solution in order to build on the value and results they achieved from their manufacturing processes. Have you thought of the additional results you could gain from a solution like this or of doing something similar?"

"In terms of the result, is your preference to gain the lowest priced solution or the lowest risk solution? The reason I ask is that we recently worked with Johnson Controls, and although they initially wanted the lowest cost solution, they felt the risks were too high. They opted for a slightly higher value, lower risk solution such as our MediaPlus package."

Create a question bank

Good questions are your loyal workers. You can use them to generate money, time after time. So keep them handy in a Question Bank where you can refer to them constantly, occasionally polish them up and make them better, or add new ones.

Status Questions	Probing Questions	Solution Questions

Use NaturalFlow™ to evolve!

By using NaturalFlow™ questioning, you will encourage a natural, more considered conversation with your customers which is by far the preference of modern day buyers. It generates trust while giving you the information you need to drive home sales.

Summary

- Questioning is still the number one skill in selling in today's market.
- The biggest benefit of effective questioning is that it reflects on you as a skilled, intelligent sales professional.
- There are questions, and there are questions that sell.
- NaturalFlow™ Questioning is a cultural shift – it helps the customer to relax and provide you with the information you need.

- Questions thrive in structure – from the general to the more specific.
- Status questions help you to understand a day in the life of your customer. Some of the status questioning techniques in this chapter, such as trigger questions, will make you money!

TIME TO EVOLVE! YOUR SALES TOOLKIT:

1. Become an expert in questioning skills – there is so much more to know. There are loads of sales resources on YouTube and Amazon, plus www.slideshare.net. Remember that just one great question can open up conversations and make you successful.
2. Role play is the finest way of honing your questioning craft. Just like Rafael Nadal keeps hitting tennis balls every day to keep his touch, so should you keep your touch by practising your questions with a colleague. Tip: Sitting back-to-back will help you to replicate a phone conversation more easily. Download our FREE Role Play Template.
3. Download our NaturalFlow™ Questioning Desk Planner to keep all of your best questions in one place.

To access the Natural Training sales resource centre for your 29 FREE resources, simply register online at www.naturaltraining.com/bonusresources

Chapter 6 – The 'Prove it to me' selling era

"If you do things well, do them better. Be daring, be first, be different, be just."
Anita Roddick

So, you've identified your prospect's needs and have established that buying is a business priority. Now, you can start to make recommendations and present a suitable solution for them to buy. However, it's important to note at this stage that the modern day buyer buys from the human face of your organisation, a Sales Maker, someone they can trust. Today, we live and work in a 'prove it' era, so what does this mean for the sales professional, and how should selling strategies be realigned to manage this demand?

We have now entered the era of 'prove it to me' selling. This has stemmed from customers watching their budgets tightly and needing some form of proof to ensure that they're going to get a return on their investment. Savvy companies know this and are doing all they can to provide that kind of proof to their prospective customers: websites are full of testimonials, case studies and video testimonials. Blogs provide prospective customers with another entry point into an organisation – a window where they can personally ask a company representative to prove a point, or a product's worth. Increasingly, companies are using real people. (You can find out more about referral-based selling in Chapter 13.)

Why are we in the 'prove it to me' era? It seems to stem from the customer's fear of the consequences of making a wrong decision. They don't want to appear foolish or ignorant by buying the wrong thing, and they're increasingly suspicious of the bias inherent in advertising, so they look to find proof that other people have bought the same product or service and been happy with the results. "Only when I see some people like me liking it, will I then like it myself."

Today's selling evolution requires this to be front of mind. When you are making a recommendation or presenting a solution to your prospect, there are two keys things that you need to include:

1) Demonstration of proof: Can you provide proof of the value and results they could gain? Instead of using the traditional "So bearing in mind that your needs are 'XYZ', I would recommend you take 'ABC' solution", you need to provide something more concrete and to position it in such a way that your modern day buyer doesn't feel as if they are being sold to.

Here's a great way to achieve this... "Let me share with you a recent story of how we helped one customer in the same field as you. If you can achieve the same value as they did, would that help you to feel more comfortable about what we are providing?" This approach reflects modern day buyer preferences: they want to make their own decision to buy rather than being sold to.

2) Outstanding value: In your trusted, evolved sales role, you need to add incredible value, be innovative and share insights. You can do this by sharing a recent customer testimonial, case study or some industry trends or triggers that are sparking new solutions for their needs. You can also ask intelligent questions (see Chapter 5 on questioning skills) around areas that your prospect may not yet have thought about. Alternatively, you could propose a new idea that you feel will turn a good solution into a great solution for the customer. This positions you as an authority figure and puts daylight between you and your competitors.

The delicate balance of insights and value

We have already established that customers are shouting out "prove it to me" in this modern sales era. You must be careful, however, not to overwhelm your customers, so finding a balance between sharing insights and suggesting new solutions is important.

HERE'S AN EXAMPLE...

Sometimes customers want a simple solution. Recently one of our customers in the engineering industry said, "I'm trying to buy a bike at the moment, but there is so much choice, and so many conflicting opinions. You know, sometimes I wish I lived in the old Soviet Union. There were two queues – if you wanted a road bike you joined the left queue, and if you wanted an off-road bike you joined the right queue. Perfect – I'll take the city one, thanks. No choice of colours? Even better!"

If you overwhelm today's already busy decision makers, it prevents them from making a decision. You could end up being the problem, rather than the solution.

When you're recommending a solution to your prospect, it really helps to understand the type of concerns or questions they may have as this will help you to find the right balance of insight and value. **Just focus on the things that will help you prove why they should buy from you, this time. This will speed up the sales process for you too.**

The natural sales evolution has meant that customers are exposed to so much choice that their heads are swimming in detail. Here's a great example of the kind of things your target customer is already thinking about when you are recommending a solution:

1. How simple is it?
2. Will it take lots of time and effort?
3. Does this person or company provide value?
4. Is it aligned to what I am trying to achieve or my business objectives?
5. Is this a priority?
6. Is it urgent?
7. Can this salesperson demonstrate and prove the results I will gain?

The point is if the customer wants proof, determine the quickest and simplest way to get them to a decision. Don't overcomplicate it.

IT'S TIME TO TALK MONEY...

Linked strongly to the 'prove it to me' sales era is price. When customers want proof, they are almost always making the connection in their mind to price. So, let's take a look at it...

There's a feeling in the sales world that customers simply buy on price - meaning salespeople tend to pitch low and offer discounts to get the deal. This does happen. However, we feel that today's customers are actually more motivated to buy low-risk high-value solutions as the fear of making a mistake and the risk element far outweigh the price. And if they don't have that feeling, then it's your job to prove it to them! A simple way to sum this up is with the statement: "Buy cheap, buy twice".

Insider Tip: To increase your confidence when pitching a higher cost solution, spend more time on questioning before moving in to the selling phase so that you can identify the true motivators for buying. You will have a stronger platform on which to base your recommendation and solution.

A GREAT STRUCTURE TO WORK WITH

A quick and easy way to prove your value to customers is by using our Challenge, Solution, Result (CSR) structure.

Challenge: What is the challenge had by a similar company to your customer? Outline it very briefly. (Take seconds not minutes!)
Solution: What solution did you provide? (Again, just a few lines, not "War and Peace"!)
Result: What results did they get?

You can come up with this type of structure in a customer conversation without any preparation. Just remember CSR!

Try your own!

Challenge	Solution	Result

HERE'S A GREAT EXAMPLE OF CSR WORKING TOGETHER...

"Katie, recently a small architect firm just like yours also had trouble selling to clients. We provided them with a high impact training programme delivered in short bursts over a month for 12 of their leading architects. In the two weeks after the training, this firm signed up two new clients and identified another two projects from existing clients worth in excess of £300,000 net revenue."

Now there's some proof! If you are going to keep evolving in this marketplace, you must integrate these types of real examples into your sales efforts. It really works.

Three more proof-based techniques

To help load up your 'proof toolbox', try using some other linguistic techniques. In our training, we give our delegates ten or so of these, but here are three of the most popular:

1) Analogies

By using analogies to cement an idea in your customer's mind, you are using an indirect method of selling that encourages rather than pushes your prospect to make a decision. You need to use analogies that you know will mean something to your prospects – for example, if you use a football analogy with a client, they better appreciate football!

2) Scenarios

Try putting your customers right into the moment by asking them to **picture** using your product or service. The simplest way to do this is by starting with the word 'imagine'. This has an impressive, sometimes hypnotic effect on people – they will actually begin to put themselves into the scenario.

HERE'S AN EXAMPLE...

"Imagine you're driving down a dark side street in London on the way to a birthday dinner. It's raining and hard to see through the fog. Worst of all, you're completely and utterly lost with no map. You think about going home, but just when you're about to turn back, you remember you have satellite navigation on your iPhone. You simply type the postcode of where you are going, and 10 minutes later, you arrive at the dinner safely!"

3) Demonstrations

"If what you are getting online is for free, you are not the customer, you are the product." Jonathan Zittrain

Product and service demonstrations are a great way to increase involvement. In the last few years, trials, tests, freemium (free, but with a premium charged for advanced features) campaigns and pilot programmes, have really grown. The reason is that we humans need to have a taster, a test drive or simply a play around to understand fully what is on offer.

Demonstrations are another way of achieving this result, because you ask your customer to become involved with your product. This level of involvement increases customer engagement and helps them to see what a day, or an hour in the life of your product looks like.

Increasingly, our clients at Natural Training are asking for training to help them demonstrate their products. It's a real growth area for us. Our clients need help because demonstrating their products to customers is more than simply 'throwing the instruction book' at them – it's more of an art form than that.

If possible, work on how to give your customers a great taste of your product via some sort of demonstration.

Here are a few tips:

- ✓ Do some quality pre-demo research – what are the likely hot buttons of your demonstration for your customer? If unsure, ask them!
- ✓ We humans love good stories, so work on the narrative as you go through. Tell the right story, mixed up with selling signposts.
- ✓ Think about certain parts where you can get the customer to 'drive' the demo. They will enjoy being behind the wheel!
- ✓ Work out how much detail is enough – and what to leave out to avoid 'feature dumping'.
- ✓ Create a strong close to your demonstration or taster. Think about commitment steps and moving them through the sales process.

Your competitors in the 'prove it to me' era

When customers are desperate for proof, they are doing so in light of a few dynamics such as price, value and quality. But there is another consideration, which is of course, your competition. You can confidently assume that 90% of the prospective customers you meet are also looking at a competitor's solutions. The power of the internet is providing today's buyers with so much choice. Barriers to entry are also lower than ever before for your competitors. There are all sorts of systems, virtual storefronts and receptions, plus great looking websites that mean competitors come from nowhere to appear on your customer's radar.

So let's look at how you can position yourself effectively as the preferred supplier against a competitor without pulling them apart and making yourself sound like a pushy salesperson (because, let's face it, there's nothing worse).

Here are a few tips to help you prove to customers that you are the better choice over your competition:

Don't slate your competitors. Denigrating your competition in front of your customer may prove only that you are confrontational and unprofessional. This is best to be avoided as it may weaken your position, not theirs.

Conduct regular research. A competitive analysis including mystery shopping is a key ingredient to staying on top of your game in the bid to prove worth against competitors.

Be aware that even if you know your solution is better than the one your prospect already has in place, don't <u>assume</u> they will move to you. Sometimes your customer will know they have an inferior product or service but don't want to do anything about it! This seems illogical to some inexperienced salespeople, and they get very frustrated.

The truth is, for most modern day buyers it's actually easier to stay with a solution that they are only 75% happy with. They view moving to your solution as time and resource heavy.

And with time being their most precious commodity, changing is not a business priority. As a result, they may delay making a decision. Your job is to make moving a business priority, break down the transition into small, manageable chunks and show them how with your help the transition will be smooth (not time consuming) and will save them a lot more time and money in the future.

Compare value and results against competitors. This is very different to slating the competition. (See the first tip) This can easily be achieved by explaining that many of the customers you meet today are also looking at competitors and that they found it very helpful when you ran a comparison for them to show them the key differentiators they would achieve.

TRY THIS: Create a table for the 'must haves' and 'nice to haves' for your prospects and then review each of the key competitors' offerings within them.

Remember, we live in a world of price comparison sites where your customers are now conditioned to seeing price as the dominant force in the sale. Not all competitors are the same; the cheap ones will be cheap for a reason.

Your customers will not only relate to you doing this exercise - they will see you as a trusted advisor who cares, adds value to their life, and who makes their decision making process easier. For this exercise to achieve the results you want, however, you must do your research first, or you could be placing the deal right into the hands of your competitors.

HERE'S A GREAT EXAMPLE...

Let's say you're selling an insurance policy. Your competitors may offer a lower entry price for the first year, which is what your customers want. However, through your research, you establish that in the second year, they actually double the premium to compensate for the first year - meaning your customers will actually pay more with your competitors over a two-year period than they would with you. You will only know this information if you do your research, and then put together a 'total cost of ownership' number for your clients. A convincing way to get the business!

Here are some more rules of engagement in today's 'prove it to me' economy:

- ✓ Do your research first.
- ✓ Come prepared with your sales toolkit including intelligent questions, testimonials, case studies, proof of results, analogies you can use, and a competitive comparison.
- ✓ Keep it simple.
- ✓ Keep it focused on them, not you.
- ✓ Add incredible value, be innovative and share insights.
- ✓ Don't oversell or overwhelm.
- ✓ Check if buying is a priority.
- ✓ Lead them – making a decision when they are already super busy is very difficult, so help by breaking the decision making process into small, manageable chunks.
- ✓ Remove their fear of buying and reduce risk.
- ✓ Be aware that today's prospects will resist change due to time pressures.
- ✓ Keep solutions, recommendations and the proposal non-complex.

Summary

- • The 'prove it to me' sales era exists because of fear of the consequences of making a poor decision.
- • Demonstration of proof and adding outstanding value will help you out in this era.

- The customer thinks about seven types of questions when you are recommending a solution.
- When they want proof, customers will be thinking around price, competitors and quality.
- Offering the right balance between insights (information overload) and value is key.
- Customers are more motivated to buy low risk, high-value solutions than they are to simply buy cheap.
- Challenge, Solution, Result (CSR) provides you with an ideal structure to prove your product to customers.
- Bring your proof to life with techniques such as analogies, scenarios and demonstrations.
- Knowing the differentiators of your competition in this era of selling is crucial.

TIME TO EVOLVE! YOUR SALES TOOLKIT:

- Download a sample case study using our Challenge, Solution, Result (CSR) format. Write one case study using CSR in the next two weeks. Aim to do at least one per month for the rest of your life after that!
- Proof is linked strongly to trust, and there is no better source for a trusted relationship than "The Trusted Advisor" by David Maister. Download some free tips from our Sales Resource Centre.
- Read "10 tips for client video testimonials" to uncover the secrets to making a great client video!

To access the Natural Training sales resource centre for your 29 FREE resources, simply register online at www.naturaltraining.com/bonusresources

Chapter 7 – Sales presentations 2.0

**"You've already tried your plan and you're
number four."**
Don Draper, *Mad Men*

*Sales professionals will present or 'pitch' the benefits of their
product or service to prospective customers at regular intervals
during their career. That's a given; it's part of the job and probably
always will be. After we uncover the needs of customers, we make
them a compelling offer. However, sales presentations too have
evolved: how we connect, engage and communicate with the
modern day buyer has changed. Importantly, the style and delivery
of our content must reflect this change. In this chapter, we look at
the various modern day methods of communicating and engaging
with prospects and the key features that exist in successful sales
presentations today.*

Years ago, delivering a sales presentation involved getting
in your car, travelling halfway across the country in
some cases and then meeting with your prospective buyers.
Baby Boomer and Generation X readers will probably
remember strapping a PC and an overhead projector to a
trolley and wheeling that into a boardroom to start a
presentation! (We're talking circa 1992, so not a million years
ago!)

Technological advances mean this kind of journey is no
longer necessary. Of course, this evolved to the PowerPoint
(PPT) era, which is still probably the dominant force today –

although we can carry both the projector and presentation on a flash drive in our pocket for under £300. (Google it, it's true!)

This chapter isn't going to be an extensive look at PPT, nor is it going to teach you the fundamentals of presenting – there are plenty of other books and courses for that. Instead, we are going to uncover what the modern day buyer wants in a presentation, and how sales has evolved (or, in many cases, hasn't evolved) to meet it. Most importantly we are going to look at what you can do to be successful.

Today's presentation platforms

Today, you need to be across much more than PPT and a boardroom table.

YOU CAN PRESENT IN MANY WAYS, INCLUDING BUT NOT LIMITED TO:

⊃ Multimedia platforms such as webinars. (Combining speech like a conference call, and slides.)
⊃ Dial in teleconferences and teleseminars (you can use these for free)
⊃ Skype (including new free technology to record and host meetings and presentations)
⊃ Social media platforms including Facebook and MSN Messenger
⊃ Dedicated boardroom video conferencing software and hardware
⊃ And more - watch this space!

As bandwidth becomes able to handle large and instant

transfer of video, expect new and exciting products to emerge that start to simulate the reality of being in a real presentation. Recently, we encountered a great example of this - http://www.kuluvalley.com/. This company offers a product that enables customers to become engaged with your product regardless of time zone. And there are loads of other video options too!

Broadly speaking, these virtual methods of communicating are becoming the new norm for sales meetings and more in line with how the modern day buyer prefers to engage. Conscious of travel budgets and environmental footprints, and with less time as a result of being asked to do more things, the modern buyer needs to push towards presentation platforms that do the same job and which are more cost effective and a lot less time consuming. And, as we know, salespeople need to evolve at least with them, and preferably ahead of the curve.

"Technology - it'll simplify a lot of tasks you never had to do before." Patrick Chapatte

The advantages of being at the vanguard of sales presenting

The communication era we have now entered opens up so much scope for sales professionals:

- ✓ You can communicate with multiple prospects at the same time.
- ✓ You can hold online meetings with clients at any time and in any part of the world – opening up opportunities that you may have previously

deemed impossible due to geographical location.

✓ You can collaborate and share information with new prospects in a whole new way.

✓ You can increase your engagement potential whilst reducing costs.

✓ You boost productivity and free up a lot more time in your diary, which means you can use that precious saved time to generate even more leads and prospects.

✓ Your presentation style and method can give you a genuine point of difference!

HERE'S AN EXAMPLE OF HOW THAT WORKS IN PRACTICE...

Natural Training went out to the marketing communications industry recently to find a partner who can help consolidate our market presence as a leading sales training brand. We received back several proposals – but one, from www.ditto.tv, was the most memorable. It was a simple video, executed beautifully, featuring head and shoulders shots of the staff of Ditto talking briefly about why they would like to do business with Natural Training. It exemplified what we were after – a progressive, video-based marketing communications company that lives and breathes the values they sell. To see the video, go here: www.naturaltraining.com/blog/2012/09/18/videoproposal

Like Ditto TV, those who embrace new methods of communication will most certainly be in a more advantageous position to traditional salespeople who will be wondering why their closing ratio is worsening!

The webinar is your new presentation ally

We all know what a seminar is – a presenter talking to a room full of people. A webinar is just that, but on screen. You see the slides, you hear and/or see the presenter, and you can interact in similar ways as you might in real life, such as asking the presenter questions and putting forward your views.

This is nothing new. Although only a few of us might be familiar with them, webinars have been around for a while now. What is new, however, is that the adoption curve is shifting. Webinars have previously been the domain of more dynamic companies in more progressive industries. Now, it is becoming a more mature market with many of your clients utilising webinars as an effective sales presentation tool.

HERE'S AN EXAMPLE...

Recently, we had a new client who enquired about a new training programme we launched, called *The Secrets of Selling to Procurement*. As it was a new programme, they wanted to see an example of the content that we would be covering and wanted to meet the trainer in advance to ensure that he would gel with their team. A few years ago, we would have sent the trainer to meet the customer to provide them with a taster session. As we are London-based and the client is Liverpool-based, this would have involved the trainer spending most of the day travelling – and since he is super busy, that wasn't an option in the short term.

Instead, we suggested that we host a one-hour webinar where our trainer would deliver a live, 45-minute taster session and then have a 15-minute Q&A session with delegates attending the webinar.

Without having the understanding and knowledge of how webinars actually operate, many assume it is just a screen and there is no opportunity for interaction. However, you can make them as interactive as you like. Webinars have evolved to encourage interaction, such as taking an online vote if attendees agree or disagree with a point you are making and allowing attendees to communicate live with the webinar host. The settings you choose to use on a webinar is completely up to you – however, we recommend that you choose your settings based on your customer's needs. As always, collaborate with the customer! Ask them in advance what level of interaction they require.

This particular customer liked our idea of hosting a webinar and was prepared to pay for it too. They were very impressed with the content we covered in the webinar and felt it was an effective use of everyone's time. The best news was we won the deal based on this initial engagement. We are now successfully deploying a blended learning solution, encompassing live face to face training, webinars and Skype coaching to develop the skills of the client's international employees - something that had not originally been included in the scope for the project.

The important lessons to learn from this approach are first, we showed the customer that we were adaptable (which, let's face it, we all have to be to suit today's buyers). Second, we were the only company out of three she had approached that wanted to use this technology. Third, it saved us a lot of time – hours and hours of it! Finally, utilising technology such as webinars is a low cost, low risk method of nurturing relationships with customers before investing time and money visiting them in person.

There is one caveat of course: the content has to be exceptional and the delivery has to be well practised and rehearsed.

Hosting a webinar alone won't win you the business – more on this later in the chapter.

Insider Tip: There are many companies now providing webinar services at either no cost or low cost that you can easily set up immediately. Many even offer a free 30-day trial and one-to-one coaching sessions to get you started. It is advisable to run your first webinar with colleagues to enable you to get comfortable with the technology. The companies that we prefer to use are: Go to Meeting (www.gotomeeting.co.uk) and Cisco webex (www.webex.com).

HERE'S ANOTHER EXAMPLE...

One of our clients, Richard, is in the Search Engine Optimisation (SEO) space. He has a small company which is brilliantly effective in the midst of many competitors making false promises about "getting you to number one on Google in two weeks".

Despite having a great product, before he came to us, Richard wasn't making money. Far from it – he was thinking of laying off people.

So we designed a strategy for him around one simple premise: we wanted to build him such an outstanding 20-minute online webinar presentation that he would win every piece of new business he went for. We wrote our goal at the top of our whiteboard in a development session with Richard: 'EVERYONE who sees this presentation will buy from Richard and his team'.

First, we needed to arrive at a theme and we chose three milestones: credibility, excitement, and the close. Richard had the first five minutes to establish that he knew what he was talking about – to gain that credibility. He had the next 10 minutes to demonstrate the product in an exciting way so that customers could SEE how it would work for them. And he had the last five minutes to close the deal.

With these three milestones in place, we built the presentation and Richard presented it to us and a few outsiders in his target market for testing purposes. We reviewed it, fine-tuned it and critiqued it. Richard worked tirelessly over two weeks to make it perfect.

There was one day, at around the two-week mark, that Richard did it perfectly. He hosted it on gotomeeting.co.uk, and his interaction, his slides, his online demos of various websites and the SEO software he uses – were all spot-on. And as clients, we loved it – we thought everyone would buy.

Then, we had to make people in his target market WANT to watch it. We felt he needed a big offer so we constructed an email for him that led with the line: "We are so confident that you will LOVE Richard's presentation on where he can take your SEO that if you are unhappy with the presentation after 20 minutes, we will give you a £100 Gordon Ramsay restaurant voucher – no questions asked."

We then bought a database of 200 Marketing and Web Managers and emailed them the offer. We had 22 replies! Richard scheduled in the dates, and presented to each person/team online, using the same web platform.

The result? 100% success! Not one person came CLOSE to asking for the restaurant voucher. Further to that, at the time of writing, 16 clients have come on board as Richard's customers. (The rest simply have to wind up their arrangement with their current supplier!)

In the stunning example above, Richard did the right thing. He invested considerable time, money and effort into perfecting his presentation. He delivered it incredibly well. He thrilled clients. And he made a big offer to get their attention – which also generated revenue for him. A perfect example of how to produce a modern say sales presentation.

Using webinar technology is an incredibly effective way of presenting and engaging with prospects. However, there are many more options.

Here are a few more, complete with some tips for success:

1) Teleconferencing:
Teleconferencing is trending up as a way to get business done – fast. Clients can dial in and interact from home, on the road, or in the office as part of their virtual team.

Some tips:

- Lateness seems to be a pandemic problem with conference dial-ins. The key is to leave yourself five minutes at the start. There are quite often dial-in and password problems, so be prepared!
- There is almost always an awkward part at the start of the call when people are joining in. There are various reasons for this: nervousness, being ill-prepared, and being late. Mitigate this by taking the lead!

- For some reason, there is a lack of structure and control with conference calls that doesn't seem to be as apparent in face to face meetings. This is possibly because everyone's status is at the same type of level with voice – there isn't the 'presence in the room' of live meetings. If you are hosting, take control! Establish who is on, who isn't, and take a social/gentle line of conversation to a couple of people. If you talk too much about work, you risk starting before the time. And in terms of control, let everyone know what it is about, what their role is, and where you need to be by the end. (Kids like surprises but adults at work do not. Always let adults know where you are taking them in a business situation.)

2) Sales presentations on Skype

We love Skype. We love the proposition (free calls with your friends around the world), the branding (light blue works well!), and the simplicity. But most of all, we love the way it helps businesses connect, develop relationships and sell.

Originally utilised by the personal user, Skype is quickly becoming an invaluable business communication tool with over 663 million registered users. Many sales professionals I know are already using Skype and are comfortable with the technology. If you are not utilising it as a way to connect, engage and communicate with prospects, you may be missing out on sales opportunities.

At Natural Training, we use Skype for two main purposes – recruitment and coaching. Adding that face-to-face dimension really helps. In addition, Skype lets you record calls (www.pamela.com) for free, as well as use features such as screen sharing, file transfers, video conference calling, call forwarding, customer service tools and more to allow your business to stay connected – internally and externally – from the ease of your computer network. If you are a small business or sole operator, you can choose a dedicated phone number for the cost of a roast dinner! It has become so natural and so vital to our business' communications that it's difficult to see our company running so smoothly without it.

So, how do you present on Skype? Here are our four top tips:

1. Alternate your eyes between your camera, and their video image, whether you are listening or talking. The camera time means that you are giving them eye contact. It takes a little practice to stare at a camera but after a while it becomes natural.

2. Be aware of your framing. We don't want to you to be so close to the camera that we can see up your nose, but equally you must take up a good part of the frame. Aim for 70% - meaning that the contents apart from you take up no more than one third of the frame.

3. Backgrounds and environment are so important. Regardless of whether at home or the office, customers need to get the right impression – meaning a clean and professional background. For example, when we were interviewing PR agencies, one chap had his washing in the background. As we were talking, we couldn't help but notice his wife's 'smalls' in the background!

4. Sound and signal strength is very important. Skype is a lot more stable these days, providing your connection is similarly

stable. Ensure you close down your busy computer applications. Skype with video takes a lot of bandwidth and processing speed, so it pays to be ready. As an extra precaution, restart your computer ten minutes before the presentation to ensure a smooth customer experience.

PLEASE DON'T FORGET THE PRESENTATION BASICS

Of course, as mentioned earlier, the caveat to all of the modern day communication methods is that you need to be able to deliver a focused, clear and memorable message within your presentations. While all this technology is great, content is king!

Here are our top five tips for presenting effectively in today's sales world, regardless of delivery media:

1. BE CUSTOMER-CENTRIC

Research has shown that the most regular complaints from audiences, in terms of sales pitches, are:

- ✘ Lacking a clear point
- ✘ Not focused enough
- ✘ Nothing beneficial in there for me
- ✘ Poorly structured
- ✘ Too confusing
- ✘ Too long

Today, it's vitally important to be on the same wavelength as the customer and let that understanding flow through the delivery. The modern customer is intolerant and has a specific desire for sales professionals to get to the point. Your mindset is important here – this pitch is not about you. It's vital that it's all about the customer.

Customers usually want FOUR questions answered:

1. What is the real value-add that I get from selecting this service?
2. Where are the relevant measurements and statistics to back up your pitch?
3. Where is the proof with appropriate testimonials or case studies?
4. How much effort has gone in to tailoring this presentation so that it's customer-centric?

Switch your focus by stepping into your client's shoes and making every effort to understand what their specific challenges are and finding out what they truly value. In reality, you could be presenting five times in one week for a particular product, but the approach you take each time is completely different because each time you allow yourself to be led by the customer.

No two are the same. Here's a nice piece of research that talks about **what clients want from a sales presentation.** Keep this on hand when you prepare your next sales presentation so that you focus on what's important:

- Previous relevant experience in our sector/category
- Track record with our organisation
- Special insights into issues/problems/audiences
- Understanding of our operating environment
- Ability to deliver solution
- Reputation
- Cost effectiveness – commitment to targets and evaluation
- Strength of senior management
- Company size and resources available

- Financial stability
- Recent new business performance
- Position with own sector
- Reputation with intermediaries
- Performance against industry surveys/benchmarks/ league tables
- Relevance of proposed solution
- Creativity of proposed solution
- Chemistry of pitching team
- Culture of company
- People and environmental policy
- Clarity of thinking and reputation for delivery
Source: Rogen

2. SMART PREPARATION

Traditionally, we prepared what we needed to say. Today, we need to prepare **how we want the customer to feel.** Traditionally, we spent time sweating while preparing a PPT. Today, we spend time focusing on a two-way interaction – a forum for collaboration. You need to prepare with some of these factors in mind.

Ask yourself these questions:

⮕ How am I getting into the minds of the people I'm presenting to?

⮕ How do I want them to *feel* at the end of my presentation?

⮕ What do I want them to do at the end of my presentation?

⮕ Have I completely pinpointed their business issues? (If not, there is still time – dial their number NOW and ask them what their issues are and what they expect from your presentation!)

The only way to answer these questions accurately is by engaging with the audience before the presentation or pitch date. There is a school of thought around a sales pitch that it has to 'surprise' the audience. Why? Your role in sales is to take out surprises (which in business are commonly called 'risks'!). Engage with your prospects, let them know your presentation structure, and check whether it suits their needs. Ask for input. It works.

Without understanding your audience completely and the outcome they want, you'll be wasting their time – they don't want that, and neither do you.

3. STRUCTURE IS KEY

When putting it all together, begin with the end in mind. While the temptation is to open a blank PowerPoint presentation document and start typing, try to resist the urge. PowerPoint isn't the right place to start. Steve Jobs, when he was running Apple, agreed: *"I hate the way people use slide presentations instead of thinking. People would confront a problem by creating a presentation. I wanted them to engage, to hash things out at the table, rather than show a bunch of slides. People who know what they're talking about don't need PowerPoint."* (Source: *Steve Jobs* by Walter Isaacson.)

Instead of slides, start with your strategy and structure. If you haven't read the previous example in this chapter about our client with the SEO company, then please do now. It's an excellent overview of how to make a winning presentation.

The key elements are:

    ✓   Work on a main goal, such as 'Position my

company with credibility'. In sales, this goal is central to you convincing the customer to say 'Yes'.

✓ Then break that down into three bite-sized pieces, such as we did in that example: credibility, excitement and the close. When you work with these smaller pieces, your presentation becomes much easier to prepare.

✓ Think of each piece as a small story or parcel of information. As with all great stories, they should have a beginning, a middle and an end.

✓ Work out where the customer can have some interaction. Maybe you can ask a question or they can provide input. *Achieving this involvement is a key to success.*

4. ACHIEVE MAXIMUM IMPACT

During our sales and presentation skills training workshops, delegates say, "I want to deliver a 'high impact' presentation but have no idea what that truly means."

What is 'high impact' NOT about? Well it's certainly not about finding fancy graphics, or sound effects. These things are nice, but they are quickly forgotten. High impact means you **change the customer's world.** To do that, you have to change the way they think about their role, their work, their industry, their strategy or their business. This is about stepping into the client's shoes and understanding what they really value. Only then can you get the 'wow' factor that you deserve.

HERE'S AN EXAMPLE...

One of our clients is a very successful designer with about 50 employees. The company was winning one in three pitches for new business, and they thought they should be winning one in two. We went along to one of their pitches and discovered that they were getting lost in detail. There was 'wow' in the pitch, definitely, but they were so caught up in discussing the tiny things – colour, fonts, white space, placement, etc. – that they forgot the bigger picture (the way the designs were going to make their 'customer's customer' feel). We refocused them on what was important, and moved elements of the detail to the Q&A (if it came up at all!). The result? In eight months, this client won eight of their ten pitches!

5. CLARITY IS KING

Despite all the current sales communication evolution, clarity remains central to everything. It's really simple; if customers don't get what you are saying, you will keep missing out on sales! It will be refreshing for your customer to know EXACTLY what you mean in a world with so many competing voices. To test clarity, run your proposition past your nine-year-old niece. If she gets it, you're on to a winner!

To summarise, you must focus on value, not detail. Drill down to what clients want to hear, not what you want to tell them. Make sure that in light of technology, you don't forget the basics of effective communication.

"A loud voice cannot compete with a clear voice, even if it's a whisper." Barry Neil Kaufman

Summary

- Sales presentations and communication have moved out of the boardroom and onto the screen.
- Presentations across many different platforms will

help you to save time and money and achieve maximum impact.

- In particular, the webinar is going to be an increasingly important ally in today's evolved presentation world.
- Teleconferencing and Skype are two important new platforms to get right.
- Don't forget the basics, such as customer-first, smart preparation, structure, impact and, of course, clarity.

TIME TO EVOLVE! YOUR SALES TOOLKIT:

1. Download our free e-book, *The Winning Pitch*.
2. Make the following promise to yourself: "I'm going to watch one TED talk every ten days for the rest of my sales career." Visit www.ted.com/talks and go on a great learning curve!
3. See if you can organise a group at work to present to each other, once a month. This is all about feedback because we never seem to get accurate feedback from customers.
4. Record your sales pitch, load it on YouTube (privately if you like) and send the link to our coaches at evolve@naturaltraining.com for some FREE expert analysis!
5. Visit our resource centre to claim your discount voucher for 20% off our open NaturalStyle 2-Day Presentation Skills workshop. Visit http://www.naturaltraining.com/training/open-courses/ for course content and scheduling.

To access the Natural Training sales resource centre for your 29 FREE resources, simply register online at www.naturaltraining.com/bonusresources

Chapter 8 - The evolved world of objections

"If I believe in something, I sell it, and I sell it hard."
Estée Lauder

Handling a prospective client's objections is part of the selling process. The mark of a successful sales professional is not strictly measured by how often prospects or customers stand in the way of closing a deal. Instead, it is measured by the way in which the seller manages those objections. The sales landscape has shifted, and the types of objections as well as the most effective way of handling them have also changed. In this chapter, we focus on how to handle today's objections and power through barriers to unearth new opportunities and new levels of success.

Your ability to handle objections successfully will define your career. Likewise, we have seen sales careers torn apart because salespeople were ill-prepared or complacent when it came to handling objections.

Today, objections are as big a problem as ever. One of the biggest ones today isn't really an objection at all – it's silence. The reason is that we don't always buy from people any more. This is born from the ease with which we are able to get quotes and receive what we need from the internet. We are becoming conditioned to not speaking to salespeople, and the increasingly impersonal nature of buying. Customers are often working from home or on the road and harder therefore to pin down. (See Chapter 4 for more about getting through to decision makers.) And maybe you don't have a relationship at all - such as dealing with Procurement. Silence is definitely a big issue, and probably the number one objection in today's world. Measure it yourself and see if you agree!

Knowledge is power

As we have learned previously in this book, today in sales, knowledge is power. Salespeople need to collect and process knowledge in a wide variety of areas to stay on top of the game. This knowledge includes, but is not limited to: buyers and their preferences; product information; competitor product information; economic factors; industrial information; and media consumption. Quite a powerful little list, isn't it?

Knowledge is particularly important when dealing with objections in the modern sales environment. Why? Well, when you're confronted with an objection from a customer or prospect, you're being handed an opportunity. Reading between the lines: regardless of the type of objection, your customer is engaged with you and the sale is moving forward. If you can handle the objection well, you move to a position of trust.

And the Natural Law of Sales #10 states that 'People buy from people they trust'.

So if knowledge is such a crucial element in dealing with objections in sales, what should the modern sales professional be doing to stay up-to-date with what's going on in the industry and the customer's world?

1. **Use Google** – Run a Google search on your customers. See where they are showing up and look out for recent announcements.

2. **LinkedIn** – Use it to find out important small details about your customer – who they know, what they know and how they came to be talking to you are all important discoveries. When you get to Chapter 12, which is all about LinkedIn, you will discover just how important this is - particularly in the B2B arena.

3. **Industry forums** – Industry forums or magazines are a great way for you to spot what's hot in your customer's industry and to find 'trigger events' that may lead to a customer objection (or help you to handle one).

4. **Plug into social media** – Twitter is an incredible resource for the modern day sales professional. Use the # function to search for the latest news on a topic relevant to your industry.

5. **Connect with your customer** – Get close to the customer by finding out what you can about them. Find out what they value most, and use this information to pre-empt objections or deal with them effectively.

6. **Competitor analysis** – This is very important in today's competitive market. If you get an objection which is based around a competitor's offering and you don't have the knowledge to handle it effectively, you might lose your trusted status. If a customer knows more about the competitive

landscape than you, they have the knowledge, and therefore the power. It's not the end of the world when customers have more power – it might make them feel good! However, it does leave you slightly vulnerable when you are put on the spot with a comment like, "But Wiggins and Co. will give me a bonus two-year guarantee".

COMMON OBJECTIONS AND TIPS ON HANDLING THEM

So what are the most common objections that sales professionals encounter? In our sales training workshops, our customers tell us the objections are: silence, price, time and "No". We have previously dealt with silence (in this chapter and also in Chapter 4 – Getting through to decision makers). Here are some thoughts on the other objections:

1) Price

There are undoubtedly some customers who will buy purely on price. There are also a lot of sales savvy modern day buyers who know that by objecting to price they can probably get the salesperson to discount their offering heavily. However, is this the customer objecting to price or is it that the salesperson wasn't properly equipped to sell value? The only real antidote to a pricing objection is value. Customers who object may well need educating in the value that you provide compared with your competitors.

Despite the customer trying to get the best deal, price objections don't always mean that price is an issue. In fact, most buyers would far prefer a high-value, low-risk solution as opposed to a low price solution - especially those motivated by fear of making a mistake or of taking a risk. As the saying goes, "Buy cheap, buy twice". To establish the real objection, you need to ask some intelligent probing questions.

2) Time
Prospects will always feel that moving from one supplier to another is a laborious and time-consuming challenge, despite sales professionals working endlessly to convince them otherwise. Also, having the time to engage with the sales professional is a common barrier in itself.

To get past the time objection, you need to make solutions or proposals as simple as possible. You need to demonstrate and prove that spending time with you will be incredibly valuable, especially if you want today's extremely busy decision makers to give you their time. Breaking any plans down into small, manageable chunks also helps.

"It takes a lot of hard work to make something simple, to truly understand the underlying challenges and come up with elegant solutions." **Steve Jobs** (Source: *Steve Jobs* by Walter Isaacson.)

3) Fifty Shades of "No"
At the time of writing there is a book that has swept the globe called *Fifty Shades of Grey*, recently voted the biggest selling book ever. Equally, in sales, there are Fifty Shades of No. As you know, "No" sometimes means "No". Sometimes, however, "No" is not an absolute "No" but a variation on the theme. There are, of course, degrees of "No".

"No" can mean:
- "No, not right now."
- "No, I can't buy it in the short term."
- "No, I can't buy it at all."

- "No, I can't buy it, but someone I know can."
- "No, I can never see myself or anyone else buying this. Go away".

Try to achieve some clarity on what "No" means. Selling today is all about feedback and altering your approach, based on what you hear and learn. Listen closely and the objections you get - every "No" will teach you how to sell.

YOUR OBJECTION HANDLING ATTITUDE IS CRUCIAL

While being equipped with the right level of knowledge and information is vital, it counts for very little unless your mind is in the right place.

Top performing sales professionals have to deal with objections, but they rarely regard them as being negative.

Don't get drawn into negativity surrounding objections - remain positive. One way you can do this is by shifting your mindset.

TAKE THIS SCENARIO...

You sell cars in a dealership showroom. It is deadline day, and you need to hit target today to get your bonus. You're feeling the pressure. Which of the following would you prefer?

1. A busy day of prospects, even though each one will have an objection around the features and functions of the cars they are interested in buying.
2. An empty showroom because no-one will walk through the door.

Of course you'd rather the busy day. You would rather be

dealing with ten customers with objections than none at all, wouldn't you? The point is to process objections as a positive, then use knowledge and relevant information to prove you can generate trust.

PURE: The Natural Training approach to handling objections

To deal with objections effectively and make them part of the journey to closing deals, you must take a considered approach. At Natural Training we have a methodology that breaks down neatly into four stages, remembered easily as PURE:

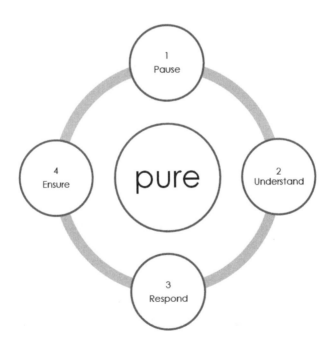

Figure 8.1: PURE objection handling

139

Stage 1: PAUSE

When you hear an objection, deploy a pause. Give yourself time to collect your thoughts and think rationally. The psychology behind this is important. The act of pausing means you avoid making a 'reactive response' (which is also known as a knee-jerk response). This is worth examining, because we believe it is one of the prime reasons for objections being poorly handled by salespeople.

In sales, we hear the same type of objections over our career, and we grow tired of hearing them and begin to treat each customer as a number, rather than as an individual. You hear the word 'price' and, like a Venus Fly Trap with its victim ready to be eaten, you jump in and move into 'fix it' mode. SNAP!

Avoid this mentality: "I must leap on the objection without hesitation because I see it as something that needs to be tackled right here and now. This objection must be quashed immediately!"

Why? We are going for a position of customer-centric sales in today's evolved selling world. The customer may feel offended by a reactive response since it shows that you aren't listening but just waiting to talk. That's a very quick way to lose the sale! It's better to pause, even if you have heard the objection 1000 times, and then respond when it's time (in this case, step 3 of PURE).

IT'S WORTH NOTING TOO THAT SOMETIMES CUSTOMERS WILL BE ABLE TO ANSWER THEIR OWN OBJECTION IF THEY ARE GIVEN SOME TIME AND SPACE, AS IN THIS EXAMPLE:

"Kelly, I don't think we can do this because we haven't got the budget (long pause as salesperson Kelly remains silent) but wait a second, maybe we can borrow some from Paul's team because he lost some headcount this year."

Stage 2: UNDERSTAND

Make sure you understand what's being asked. If you don't know what's being asked, how are you going to answer their questions properly? You can seriously let yourself down at this stage if you rush and try to resolve the wrong issue. There is also a need to clarify the specific objection before responding. For example, a customer could say "It's too expensive" but "expensive" could mean any number of things: "Too much to pay right now but could pay it next month" or "I can't see the value". To clarify what your customer means by "expensive", you need to ask probing questions before answering. There is a significant part of this book dedicated to probing questions because we feel they are a key part of your sales skills (see Chapter 5 on *Questioning*).

Stage 3: RESPOND

Usually the objection IS a genuine one, and it DOES come from the right place. And most of all, it is unique and natural to your customer. So, empathy is crucial. Use important phrases like, "I can understand how that is an issue for you." (And MEAN it, don't just say it and move on to your answer).

When you handle the objection, remember that 'fixing' it is secondary to listening and responding from the right place. If you can help your customer with their concern on the spot, then do so. If you can't, or don't want to commit, then it is

141

fine to put a plan into place to do so later. You might have to confirm some details with your Manager for instance. Either way, when you do respond, do so with empathy and sincerity and be calm and considered.

Stage 4: ENSURE

Have you answered the query correctly and offered the customer everything they need to get back on track and move forward with the sale? In this final stage, you are **ensuring** that everything is cleared up, and that your customer is happy with your answer and they have no further objections.

A sweeper question might be useful here: "Ciara, is there anything else?" Your job is to 'milk out' all the objections so that you clear the way for a smooth sale. If there are any hidden or final objections, then it's your job to know them, and deal with them.

Using this four-stage technique, you can be sure that objections are handled professionally, giving you the maximum chance of success.

HERE'S AN EXAMPLE OF HANDLING OBJECTIONS IN PRACTICE...

Situation:
An office cleaning sales professional has worked hard at a proposal and is confident that the prospect is keen to move forward with the sale. At the last minute, they get a phone call from the decision maker explaining that they have decided not to go with the proposal, based on price.

Solution:
Pause - Your key understanding is that this deal has hit a

barrier because of price. It may be that the price is too high because of the company's financial situation. Maybe they are comparing you to another supplier that's cheaper. Gather your thoughts and, in your mind, create some probing questions to establish the true objection. The point is, don't just start talking! Take a deep breath, and seek first to understand.

Understand - Before you suggest anything, you need to find out the real objection. You do this by asking questions such as, "Can I just check exactly what it was about the price that led you to make this decision?"

Listen actively for the answer and identify detail. If it's comparative, then you have to find out exactly what the rival company is offering in terms of all the variables that go into a cleaning solution. Does their offer include meticulous cleaning of keyboards and computer peripherals? Does it include bathrooms and the kitchen? What are the contract terms – how long are they asking for a rolling commitment? Once you have identified the specific points of difference in both offerings, you can focus attention on just the areas that matter.

If it's that they don't see it as a good investment for the money, you need to go back into your questioning stage and find out exactly what they do see as a good ROI and what value they would need to see. Maybe you need to find out exactly what they seek to gain, and what pain they seek to avoid with your more thorough office cleaning offer.

Respond: When you do have the right detail, you can respond appropriately and with real empathy. For the purpose of this exercise, let's say the real objection was that they simply wanted to try to get a better deal and a discount. In the current climate, this has become particularly prevalent.

After asking your probing questions, you identify that they do see the true value and they do have the budget, but they need to feel as if they have gained the best deal.

BEARING THIS IS MIND, YOUR RESPONSE WOULD BE:

"Gareth, I understand what you're saying. We have lots of customers today who are also trying to make the most of every penny they spend. Here's an idea that I think you will like: instead of discounting the price or removing some of the quality that we initially had in the solution, I would rather add some more value for you. How about we offer you our famous yearly Spring Clean, usually priced at £1200, for half price? This gives you a much better deal in terms of what you are getting for the money, and it will enable you to have a sustainable long-term cleaning solution rather than just short-term results. What do you say?"

Ensure: This is where you now need to close the objection and move on. For the purpose of the exercise, assume they have said "Maybe". Ah - this is still not a closed deal! You need to find out what "maybe" means - more probing and questioning is needed to ENSURE that you have handled the objection effectively. Don't forget your sweeper question: "Is there anything else?" Once you have cleared away their final objections and negotiation points, it's time to close, to ENSURE you have the deal!

"Providing there isn't anything else Gareth, can you confirm that you will be able to sign this off today – providing we give you this additional fantastic value?"

You have successfully handled the objection, and you didn't have to discount. Adding value rather than discounting is not only better for your bottom line, it's better for your customer too!

Summary

- Your ability to handle objections effectively will define your sales career.
- Your mindset needs to be positive - objections demonstrate engagement.
- Knowledge is power – use the resources at your fingertips to be prepared.
- A considered approach to objections is better than a reactive response.
- The three biggest objections are still the same: price, time and "No".
- Handle your objections with the Natural PURE system – Pause, Understand, Respond, and Ensure.
- Facts, figures, and demonstrations (case studies, testimonials) are vital tools in handling objections.

TIME TO EVOLVE! YOUR SALES TOOLKIT:

- Utilise our PURE objection handling worksheet to become more proficient at handling objections in today's evolved market place.
- Go to YouTube and Slideshare.net and search on objection handling. There are hundreds of small tips such as nuances of language that can really help.
- Prioritise objection handling as an agenda item in your regular team sales meetings.
- Do you have particularly hard to solve or manage

objections? Book a team taster session with our objection handling expert – claim your discount voucher by visiting our Sales Resource Centre.

To access the Natural Training sales resource centre for your 29 FREE resources, simply register online at www.naturaltraining.com/bonusresources

Chapter 9 - Modern day negotiation skills and techniques

"If you don't know where you're going, any road will get you there."
Lewis Carroll

In previous chapters, we've established that sales has evolved to focus on customers and their increased level of sophistication. With this customer-centric focus comes some wonderful advantages, such as your customer feeling valued, empowered and more confident. The downside however is clear – your customers are now in a much better position to negotiate based on transparency of prices driven by web properties such as price-comparison websites. In this chapter, we examine what the sales evolution means for today's salespeople looking to protect revenue margins.

"Whatever price you offer me, I can get a better one somewhere else." If this is the mindset of today's customer, targeting price and value at the negotiation stage, how do effective selling strategies manage this point of the sale? As always at Natural Training, we start with the mindset of the customer – in this case, today's modern negotiator.

SUCCESSFUL NEGOTIATORS DEMONSTRATE THREE CRUCIAL QUALITIES, WHICH ARE:

1. Curiosity: delving deeper into the how's and why's of the negotiation.

2.   Optimism: not developing a rapid, negative emotional response to smokescreen comments about the 'economic environment', for example.
3.   Resilience: always keeping the prize in mind!

Then during the negotiation process, these same individuals will:

✓   Carry out extensive planning and preparation (with the greatest research tool ever known to man: the internet).
✓   Be able to build rapport with customers.
✓   Manage and handle other parties' road blocks and dirty tricks.

Ponder these changes for a moment in light of the natural sales evolution! If 15 years ago, customers were being bullied into pricing submission, now look at their talents and abilities. Today's modern seller, a Sales Maker, has to be so much more prepared.

There are other forces that come into play in today's natural sales evolution too!

Have you thought about some of these?

➲   Remote working, which means negotiations now happen a lot more with individuals around the globe, rather than teams around a boardroom table.
➲   Communication, which means negotiations are now more likely to happen during conference calls, Skype and Webex meetings than face to face.
➲   Procurement and Buying Agencies, comprised of professional negotiators who come in right at the end of the sale, trying to get you focused solely on

pricing reductions.
⮑ Information overload, which means customers know exactly how much to pay and what your hot buttons are, probably before you even know they exist! Negotiations therefore start much earlier in the sale, as pricing is on the table earlier.

Let's look at some of the hot topics in today's negotiation arena, starting with our good friend – price!

Price – it's like the weather!

When strangers are meeting for the first time, they try to find some common ground to talk about. Kids, sport, and of course the weather are big, because there is the greatest chance of the other party being able to contribute to the conversation. Price is a bit like the weather. It's a common denominator – everyone relates to it. That's why your customers bring up price unusually early in the sale: they have a degree of comfort about it. They might not know what a Content Management System does, but they do know that 12 occurs after 11 and before 13. So when you are selling today, you have to understand this pricing mindset and deal with it confidently by refocusing the customer on what they need to know before you move on to price.

PRICE ATTACK!

It's always been the case that salespeople are attacked on the issue of price. We know this at Natural Training because we hear it all the time – salespeople give 'price' as the number one reason why customers aren't interested, or say "No". What sets today's successful sales professionals apart is their mindset. They have to make the decision about themselves, and ask: "How assertive am I going to be in this situation? Am I going to enter into this early price discussion, which is where the customer wants me to go, or am I going to trust my sales process and my product, and play this out the way I want to do it?" In any given market, there will be those individuals who only want to focus on price. Don't join them in a rapid race to the bottom of your rate card.

As part of your preparation going into the negotiation, you need to decide whether you are prepared to play that pricing game or not.

Remember, no buyer is going to say "Yes" to your first offer! They want to get the lowest price possible out of you, so will push for the best deal they can get. You must go into the negotiation with the end in mind. The buyer has their optimum price, so what's yours?

IT'S REALLY ABOUT VALUE!

Recently, we had a client who was dealing with one of the major airlines. We asked whether he had closed the deal. His response? "They haven't said 'No'; they just can't decide."

Sound familiar? There might be a few reasons for this, but one of the primary ones is value.

If customers can't see your value smacking them in the face, then they probably won't buy.

Value is the lubricant that is oiling the wheels of today's successful salespeople. As the seller, you need to focus on the different components that make up your offer and decide where the added value is and where the variables are. If you haven't done this exercise recently, or at all, then do it now! Bring it up in your weekly sales meeting. Ask your Manager, "What is our value for customers relative to our competition?" (Remember if everyone is offering the same value then it's not true, differentiated value). If your Manager doesn't have the answers, go further afield. Ask your marketing people, the Directors, the product specialists – and compare answers. You will come up with a value set – sometimes we call this a 'value bank' – that will help customers to see the value you are delivering.

A final point on value, because it is explored more thoroughly in Chapter 3 of this book: value means different things to different customers. A dying man in a desert will value a glass of water much more than you value the glass of water in front of you right now. Keep that in mind during your negotiations, and ask, "What value do we have that will work for this particular customer?" For example, sometimes a customer is after the 'best'. For some customers, best means 'most expensive' (yes, some people simply want to pay more!). For others, 'best' means finest quality. Value comes to the ball dressed as many things, with many interpretations. Understand it (via great questions), then sell on the customer's perception of value. It works.

THE PERFECT EXAMPLE OF THIS COMES VIA A STORY FROM AMERICAN SALES GURU BRIAN TRACY. HERE IS THE STORY AS WE REMEMBER IT:

A man and his wife met a real estate agent outside an impressive-looking two-storey property. The husband had warned his wife about displaying too many buying signals - he saw it as his role to talk down the value of the house from the moment he entered. The agent took the unusual yet highly effective step of taking them around the back door of the house, which faced a beautiful garden.

"Oh dear God!" exclaimed the wife. "Look at that beautiful flowering cherry tree. I used to have one just like that when I was growing up. We used to play under it until the sun went down. It was just like this one!" They then entered the lounge-room. "A bit small," said the husband, "and I don't think there's enough natural light." "However," the agent replied, turning to the window, "look at the view onto that beautiful flowering cherry tree." The wife stood mesmerised, gazing at the tree.

Then they went into the kitchen.

"Needs a facelift," grumbled the husband (no doubt sensing a shift in power!). The wife barely noticed – she was staring out the window at the beautiful flowering cherry tree.

"Quite a view isn't it?" chuckled the agent. "Can you imagine the kids swinging off the lower branches?"

And so on throughout the house, with the agent countering the husband's complaints with more references to the beautiful flowering cherry tree. They hadn't even looked at the upstairs rooms, but the agent knew the house was all but sold, and the husband sensed that they would be paying the asking price. All because of a tree!

Note in this story the agent's razor-sharp focus on the one piece of value that made that house distinct from any other. The agent was clever because he saw little point in talking about the other features of the house. And the husband, seeing this unfold in front of him, was powerless because of the emotional attachment his wife had to the cherry tree.

When you are in your next negotiation, think of the following memory hook: "What is the flowering cherry tree for my customer?" If you don't know it, find out – it will make you money!

Preparation is the key!

All of this pre-negotiation work is your **preparation phase.** Putting in the groundwork before you engage with a customer at the negotiation table is vital. You know that the customer will be focused on price (cost/budget) for the reasons we have discussed. They will also bring in some competition, real or fake. You know that too. This is, in fact, one of the key tricks played by customers – more on that later.

In terms of preparation, you need to conduct effective analysis on your customer and ascertain where their true motivations, desires, needs and pressures lie.

At Natural Training, we have a Negotiation Dashboard to help you prepare (see your end of chapter toolkit). What is it that they want to get out of the negotiation, and where does your power lie? This boils down to buyer analysis. Let's not kid ourselves, if you're selling something to a company, the chances are you're up against three, four, or maybe more sales teams competing for the same business.

The level at which you analyse the buyer in your prep work can make the difference between closing that deal and going home empty-handed. To the buyer, there may be very little difference between you and your competitors. The secret is to know what those differences are!

Let's split the buyer analysis into three parts:

1.   The motivation to buy. What specifically is driving the person sitting opposite you? What is fuelling their investment of time in you?
2.   The technical side. What particular business purpose will the purchase of your product or service achieve?
3.   The commercial side. The price and the available discounts.

LET'S LOOK AT AN EXAMPLE OF HOW THIS WORKS...

I'm the CEO of a small business and I'm in the market for a new office. I want a bigger office as my staff has outgrown the last place and I also want to work closer to my customers in the Cambridge area of the UK. Money is, of course, an issue and although I want to move, I can hold out for the right price.

Commercial estate agents are keen to take me to viewings. I wonder if they have conducted any buyer analysis on me?

Here are my considerations: (See Fig 9.1 on following page.)

*   Motivation: Bigger office, more prestigious area (this is the emotion).
*   Technical side: Accommodate growing staff (this is the logic).
*   Commercial side: Cost is a concern and I will sacrifice the speed of the move to find the right price (this is the money).

What this kind of simple analysis does is help you to build a profile of your customer. Remember, it's far easier to build rapport with someone when you know more about them. How much better prepared would a commercial agent be knowing those three simple considerations?

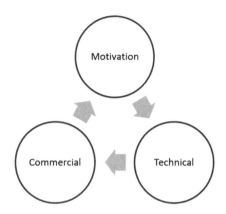

Fig 9.1: The three considerations of buyers

All they have to do is ask! Yet this is based on a real event, and the person in this case study was stunned by the lack of questions directed towards her. Agents simply didn't try to find out what her motivation, technical and commercial considerations were!

The reality is that negotiation is increasingly becoming about your interpersonal skills. It becomes far easier to build rapport with a customer once you know more about them and what it is they're after. As we have emphasised in previous chapters, the role of sales professionals has evolved. Customers are empowered with information, so now you are important as the human face of the business transaction – a Sales Maker! You need to make them like you, make them feel good about themselves, make them see your value, and make them buy! This is summed up in that wonderful word 'rapport'.

A good salesperson will make a prospective customer feel good about the product, but a great salesperson will make customers feel great about themselves.

It's all about style!

In today's negotiation world, we have to be hyper-aware of the styles that others bring into play. There are different styles or approaches to the negotiation, and the top performing salespeople have carried out enough research on their customer to know exactly which ones to adopt to get the result they require. Today's styles have evolved because of the environment in which we work.

They are, in no particular order:

1. Partnering style. This person will work with you to get the best result. The partnering negotiator will be a team player, so sit on the same side of the desk, real or virtual, as them and enjoy the win-win environment!

2. Jousting style. With this person, you need to engage in the battle and compete for the best price. The natural sales evolution means that this person may well be part of a Procurement function and be logic driven. (See Chapter 10 for more on selling to Procurement.)

3. Avoiding style. This person wants to avoid confrontation or a heated debate. Help this person by focusing on the benefits and the goal of the negotiation. It's worth noting that today's customer environment is heavy on information, which may have the effect of tiring out a customer by the time the negotiation stage is reached. Tired of choice, they may just want to get the deal done! You need to recognise this and work with them.

4. Accommodating style. Create a 'Yes' environment where you try to do as much as you can for the customer. They want to work with you, so get cracking! Use the resources available to you (for example, case studies and testimonials) to expedite the decision.

5. Compromising style. Meeting in the middle is the best course of action with this style. It's like the Collaborative style, but focused more on the result than the process of working together. For this style, understand what variables you have to put on the table and be willing to show them that you are willing to bend – providing you get something back! Don't forget that value comes to the party dressed as many things – you need to look around and the natural sales evolution will provide you with as many resources as you need, such as PDFs, videos and invitations to events, to make the customer feel valued.

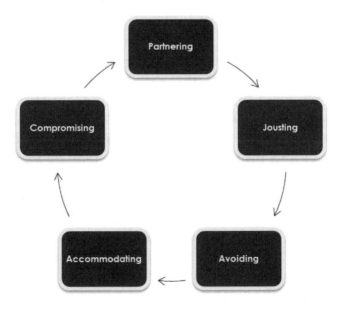

Fig 9.2: The five natural negotiation styles

Negotiation variables have evolved too

The best negotiators know which variables they can utilise that are perceived as high value to the customer but low cost to them. In the age of 'Freemium', this has never been more true. Customers have a wide variety of free, or close to free, ways to sample suppliers now – and this sampling trend is growing, from free newspapers on train networks around the globe, to the voucher phenomenon. Let's have a look at some of the variables that allow sales professionals to walk away from the negotiation table with maximum reward for their efforts...

HERE'S A GREAT EXAMPLE...

Negotiating with low cost variables is a key feature of an effective selling strategy. The software industry is particularly reliant on variables to differentiate their offering in the light of competition. One of our customers in a hugely competitive segment of the software market found its salespeople were frequently hitting the negotiation table with large companies. As always, they were trying to offer the best deal while holding on to some commission for themselves and profit for the business. One day during a meeting, one of the salespeople asked a direct question: "What would you truly value to make this deal happen?" The customer, slightly taken back, replied: "We have been burned in the past by another supplier, and an expensive roll-out. Now we need this software to work well and for us to get maximum return in the shortest space of time to restore faith in the business."

So the customer simply wanted assurance that the software would do what the sales team said it could do! Finally, the sales team sealed the deal with: "How about free support training so that we can encourage a surge in initial adoption of the software? Some sharp, focused training sessions will help everyone understand how the software works and how to get maximum return. It will cost you nothing, except a few hours of your time."

The customer agreed, and the deal was done. In this example, we have great listening skills and problem solving abilities. But we also have an example of how a low-cost high- value variable enabled the sales team to maximise their return on a deal that looked as if it would never close.

How many variables can you identify within the products or services that you sell? In the left column, list the variables – for example, 'training'. In the right column, put the benefit, such as 'increases adoption of the software'.

Product Variables	Benefit to customer

Now, name the top three variables from the list that offer low cost to you but high value to your customer. This is a great exercise to help you to maximise your value when negotiating. (See table on next page to write your answers.)

1.
2.
3.

The conditional request statement

Even the order in which we structure our sentences can swing control back to the buyer. The conditional request statement is a great example of how this works.

The conditional request statement is the age-old "If you do something for me then I will do something for you" agreement. Today, these statements have evolved with subtleties that the skilled negotiator will pick up.

Note the slight difference in the following two sentences:

1. "If I were to consider reducing the price, would you be prepared to sign the contract today?"
2. "If you can sign the contract today, we can think about moving on the price."

In sentence two, the salesperson is clear as to what they want the customer to do before making a change to the price. In sentence one, the option to move on price (which is what the buyer wants to do) is mentioned right at the start – the power shifts to the buyer and all they will focus on is driving down cost.

Know the differences and the subtleties in language in a negotiation. Trained buyers will spot this immediately and use it against an inexperienced or untrained salesperson. Don't let that be you!

Finally, Natural Training's Eight Negotiation Principles to help guide you in today's tough market:

1. Negotiation is VALUE. At the heart of every negotiation sits value: maximising it, articulating it, adding it and protecting it.
2. Negotiation is RELATIONSHIPS. People are more likely to buy from people who they relate to so don't forget the human component!
3. Negotiation is PLAYING. You need to explore the outer edges, which is the dance and fun of negotiation. Operating in a comfortable middle ground can be too dominant as a strategy.
4. Negotiation is UNDERSTANDING. Understanding is the lifeblood of your negotiation. Consultation skills are the key to this (not simply 'haggling', as many believe).
5. Negotiation is EXPOSURE. The more you negotiate, the better you are. Expose yourself to negotiations and reap the reward of experience.
6. Negotiation is PLANNING. The successful negotiator is well planned. Imagine the likely twists and turns, objections, decision making power and likely outcomes.
7. Negotiation is SOLVING. Thinking of creative new ways to solve old problems is integral to negotiating.
8. Negotiation is COURAGE. Knowing when to sit and when to play are hallmarks of today's courageous negotiator.

Summary

- Your customers today are set up to negotiate great value for themselves – you likewise need to evolve.
- Today's successful negotiators will be curious, optimistic and resilient.
- Understand the price : value dynamic. Value must smack the customer in the face.
- Keep the story of 'the flowering cherry tree' front of mind.
- Understanding your buyer is key – motivation, technical and commercial buyers.
- The five negotiation styles are important as they drive most negotiations.
- Negotiation variables and conditional request statements are important to learn and apply.

TIME TO EVOLVE! YOUR SALES TOOLKIT:

1. Prepare more thoroughly for your next negotiation by downloading Natural Training's Negotiation Dashboard from our Sales Resource Centre. Spend 15-20 minutes using the dashboard to safeguard against unnecessary twists and turns in your negotiation.

2. Use role play with a colleague before your next negotiation to ensure that you are considering all issues, angles, moods and preferences.

3. Negotiation is a complex subject with many different strategies, which makes it endlessly interesting. Commit yourself to consuming 20 minutes per week of quality negotiation information from sources including Amazon, SlideShare and YouTube.

4. Don't forget to read the chapter on Selling to Procurement – this is where you have to bring some considerable negotiation talents to the table.

To access the Natural Training sales resource centre for your 29 FREE resources, simply register online at www.naturaltraining.com/bonusresources

Chapter 10 - The secrets of selling to Procurement

"If you can stay calm while all around you is chaos, then you probably haven't completely understood the situation."
Spotted on a t-shirt in Rome

We have entered the era of Procurement and Buying Agencies! Your customers are realising that effective Procurement teams can make substantial business savings by squeezing the margins of under-prepared and inexperienced sales professionals. In this chapter, we take a look at how you can make sure you're not easy prey for Procurement. We reveal insights into the Procurement world and offer practical steps to help you understand how this cost-driven department is structured and how you can turn the tables and know when to hold your price.

The vast majority of sales professionals have been through training programmes in the art of negotiation, building rapport, selling value, or something similar. It's all important stuff, but when we talk about selling to Procurement, it's the sales professionals who can understand and unravel the strategy of their customer who will find success.

How well do you understand the Procurement process?

It's only once you understand the strategy that Procurement professionals use to drive up value and squeeze your margin that you feel capable of 'playing the game' on a level surface. This is a power struggle. The salespeople who know how Procurement operates, what they are thinking, what they are looking for, how best to engage in negotiation with them, and even how best to bypass them, are far better equipped to make the sale.

With that in mind, let's unpack the world of Procurement and see what makes them tick!

PRICE IS NOT ALWAYS THE PROCUREMENT PRIORITY

It should come as no surprise that Procurement is measured on savings and, as we all know, 'what gets measured gets done'. Price is very important but it's not always the priority.

When it is all about price, sales have been commoditised (made to be 'everyday', like petrol prices) and you have little choice except to allow your price to be squeezed. Procurement know that perception is more important than reality – they know that if you believe that the sale is all about price, they have won and you will allow your margin to be squeezed. Procurement will therefore do everything they can to convince you of this.

You, the sales professional, should remember that when this power struggle is not just based on price, you have two options:

1. Beat Procurement. These professional buyers can be weak in certain areas. You need to identify where these areas are and then exploit them.
2. Collaborate. When Procurement is stronger, you should find ways to work with it on the financial side, and help to remove supply chain costs.

166

THE TOP CHALLENGES FOR SALES PROFESSIONALS WHEN SELLING TO PROCUREMENT

There's nothing worse than feeling as if you've made the sale, after months of hard work, only to find the deal being held up by the Procurement team of the company you're selling into. Today, with Procurement becoming an important asset to any business and with many earning bonuses that directly correlate to the savings they generate, dealing with them can be tough.

Let's be clear about the top challenges that you will face when you come up against professional buyers in the Procurement team.

Psychological: Many salespeople go into Procurement feeling weak. If you feel that you have very little chance of actually succeeding, the chances are you won't.

Value selling: Not knowing how to sell value to Procurement is the second main challenge. As a sales professional, you may be trained to sell value from your own side, but you also need to understand the environment of Procurement and how they perceive value. (See Chapter 3 on developing a value proposition.)

Calling the bluff: A key challenge is also knowing when Procurement is bluffing. Despite the officious tone, and the contractual arrangements which are 'set in stone', and the specialised language, they do bluff - regularly. You need to be empowered to make the sale and to do this you need to know your price is right. If you know when Procurement is bluffing, you'll know to stay and fight on. But, how can you tell when to bring down the price or when to stick? That's the tricky part – and that's what we will be exploring throughout this chapter.

Getting your prep right for Procurement

Prepping ahead of meetings and negotiations with Procurement is critical and will help to determine how successful you are in terms of closing the sale with a healthy profit margin. Remember that Procurement is likely to also be personally motivated by the amount of money they save their employer, and will undoubtedly be preparing to engage with you and spot any weaknesses in your proposal.

One important stage of this preparation is ascertaining who it is you're working with, because Procurement can vary from business to business.

Essentially, the department has evolved in stages and different businesses will be at different points of this evolution. The key is to work out where the Procurement team that you are working with is in terms of development.

Here are the four stages:

1. **Admin and control:** Operational function to ensure the right money goes to the right supplier. This is the very early development stage of Procurement. This is purely a functional role.
2. **Secure supply:** By dealing with suppliers, the Procurement team merely keeps the factory or workspace running effectively.
3. **Bottom line savings:** In this evolution, there is recognition of the actual cost-saving potential of Procurement. Companies at the third stage of development will also appreciate, or will have seen,

the massive impact that the Procurement team can have on profitability.

4. **Top line added value:** The most developed stage recognises that Procurement plays a very important role in adding value to their customers.

From a sales perspective, it is difficult to bypass Procurement today. What's important is to work out where the Procurement Department sits in terms of the evolutionary cycle described above. This should be a huge part of your preparation period:

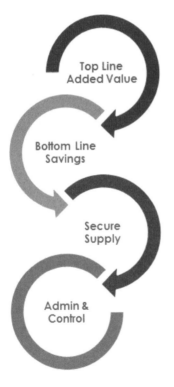

Fig 10.1: The evolution of Procurement

- Procurement people from an Admin & Control focus will have very different goals to those with a Top Line focus, so you should focus on adding value accordingly. With those from the Admin & Control stage, you need to ensure the order and delivery process is efficient.
- With those from the Secure Supply stage, you need to ensure the product or service is delivered on time to specification.
- With those from the Bottom Line Savings stage, you need to ensure Procurement can

169

show a saving, either from last year's price or your original offer.

- With those from the Top Line Added Value stage, you need to take extra care to ensure you understand and meet Procurement's stakeholder's needs.

Determining Procurement's current status should be a significant part of your preparation period.

WHAT'S THE ONE THING PROCUREMENT HAS THAT YOU HAVEN'T?

Sales professionals are at a disadvantage because Procurement uses a tool that most sales professionals aren't aware of, let alone know how to use. This tool sits at the heart of all Procurement decisions. By fully understanding the workings of this tool, you can not only negate Procurement's advantage, but go further and turn it into one of your most effective sales tools. Big claim? Let's make it come true...

We are pleased to say we can share this tool with you. It's a matrix, called the Kraljic Portfolio Purchasing Model, which was originally developed by Peter Kraljic who sits on various Boards today (try Googling some of his work).

The matrix really is the Procurement bible

Every Procurement Manager will use this matrix as a base and, in every team, the Manager or Director will map out for the whole company where suppliers are sitting in the matrix. (See Fig 10.2 on next page.)

As with most effective matrices, the beauty lies in its

simplicity. As you can see, the Kraljic matrix consists of two axes: Category Spend and Supply Risk.

Procurement uses the 80/20 rule to determine Category Spend. Which means the highest spending categories (products and services) sit above the line and in number represent about 20% of the categories, but 80% of the total relative spend.

Determining Supply Risk is a little more complicated. The level of Supply Risk is a function of the category's internal criticality/complexity and external supply chain challenges. One of Procurement's key tasks is to lower this Supply Risk.

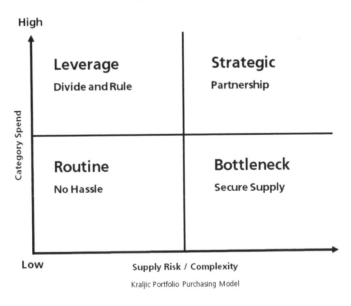

Fig 10.2: The Kraljic Matrix

THESE QUADRANTS DRIVE THE CATEGORY STRATEGY

Procurement is then able to position categories on the matrix according to their Category Spend and Supply Risk.

171

The quadrant in which the product or service falls, determines its strategy:

Leverage (top left)

- **Factors:** High spend, low supply risk.
- **Power:** Is with Procurement.
- **Example:** An example for a manufacturer might be sheet metal where the specifications are industry standard, the supply chain is well managed and several suppliers have been approved.
- **Strategy:** Procurement can play the market and drive prices down, hence the 'Divide and Rule' label.

Strategic (top right)

- **Factors:** High spend, high supply risk.
- **Power:** Is shared.
- **Example:** A bank might outsource its IT department where the spend is high and the effectiveness of its IT is critical to the running of the business.
- **Strategy:** Procurement will be looking for close relationships in order to remove costs and add value, hence the 'Partnering' label.

Bottleneck (bottom right)

- **Factors:** Low spend, high supply risk.
- **Power:** Is with sales.
- **Example:** A chemical producer might need maintenance of a specialist machine where the spend is low, the choice of suppliers is limited and the continued functioning is process critical.
- **Strategy:** Procurement will be looking to 'secure supply' by managing inventory and agreeing long-term contracts.

Routine (bottom left)

- **Factors:** Low spend, low supply risk.
- **Power:** Shared.
- **Example:** A supermarket chain might need temporary office labour where the spend is low, the skills are standardised and availability is high.
- **Strategy:** Procurement will be looking to 'secure supply' by managing time and money spent on acquisition by process efficiency, product standardisation and supplier reduction, hence the 'Routine' label.

When you use the matrix and plot out where they are likely to see you, you will immediately be empowered and, therefore, in a far stronger position.

By understanding the matrix, you can understand when Procurement is bluffing - when price is not actually its priority. This will enable you to dilute the power of these professional buyers who are constantly trying to squeeze your margins.

Knowing where you sit on the matrix is not always easy, but you should already have much of the required information. You should know whether you are a large supplier to Procurement, whether Procurement's stakeholders see value in your offering, how many real competitors you have, and how easy it is for your customer to change suppliers, etc. And if you don't know, just ask! Work out some questions that will help you to get to the truth.

Remember that to build an accurate picture, you need to go further and wider than just Procurement.

If they won't answer your questions, find someone who will. It could be worth a lot of money to you to find out where you truly sit within the matrix.

As you've seen, the matrix is a great tool for Procurement. But once fully understood, it has even more power as a sales tool. This is the control part, because successful selling strategies actually use the matrix to form counter-strategies. So, you get to a point where you can say, "Let's not look at this as a Procurement tool; let's look at it as a sales tool." Then you can really focus on how you manage Procurement, how you get the highest margin, and how you move them around the matrix – rather than the other way around. These advanced strategies are covered in our *Secrets of selling to Procurement* training seminars and workshops.

The matrix empowers Sales to focus on customers where the margin will be largest. For example, you now know that in Leverage, you are weak, Procurement doesn't see your value and has plenty of willing suppliers. Due to the high spend in this category Procurement is highly motivated to achieve savings. Here, you can only expect a low, or perhaps even non-existent, margin. Ask yourself, "Is this where we really want to spend our sales resources?"

Conversely, in Bottleneck, you have a customer who needs you. In fact, they have very little choice but to use you! Furthermore, they are not at all focused on the price (yes, it does happen). The question you need to ask here is: "Are we charging enough?"

PROCUREMENT IS ABOUT CONTROL

Whoever is driving the pricing negotiation will more than

likely emerge with the bigger smile on their face when the contracts are signed. Knowledge is power, and the more power you have going to the negotiation table with Procurement, the more chance you have of driving a successful outcome.

HERE'S AN EXAMPLE OF HOW UNDERSTANDING THE PROCUREMENT MATRIX CAN SUPPORT SALES...

Sales professionals and sales teams always come back to us with positive messages about margins or increased sales following sales training that investigates the matrix system that Procurement uses. One company we recently trained actually increased their margins by understanding the matrix. This was interesting because this was a sales team that had believed it was in a strong position, having regular sales, good margins and great customer relationships. The problem was while the sales team believed it was in a strong position, it had no point of comparison.

By understanding the matrix, the team could see just how powerful their position was. The truth was, they could be charging more, and that was the case for the majority of their products. It came to light that the customers had very little choice in terms of alternative places to purchase. The sales team were in a powerful position, but they weren't optimising that position and making the most of it. With our help, they did optimise that position and, as a result, revenue grew.

Summary

- Procurement and buying agencies have evolved to become a major force in most sales – this affects you!

- Procurement will attempt to focus you on price. You need to ensure that you can play their game, by understanding what they know.
- There are four evolutionary stages of Procurement – you need to recognise each stage and how it impacts you.
- The matrix that all Procurement professionals use is an essential tool to know and use.
- Utilise the matrix well and you can turn the tables on Procurement and play them at their own game.
- It's possible to turn the tables and make the Procurement matrix a sales tool to help you protect your revenue margins.

TIME TO EVOLVE! YOUR SALES TOOLKIT:

1. Complete our Procurement Profiler and become an expert in what Procurement people do by understanding their job role and what they value.
2. Download our interview with Procurement expert Sean Sydney as he gives you insights into how to deal with Procurement.
3. The Kraljic Matrix is your new weapon in the fight to maintain your profit margins when pitted against Procurement and buying agencies. Utilise our worksheet to help strategise for your next big encounter.
4. As always, take control of your own learning by Googling this topic and seeing the various resources including videos that are available.

To access the Natural Training sales resource centre for your 29 FREE resources, simply register online at www.naturaltraining.com/bonusresources

Chapter 11 - The 'online to offline' sales conversion strategy

"Almost any mistake you can make in running a company, I've probably made."
Mark Zuckerberg

The latest era of the internet, along with other evolving multimedia platforms, has brought new potential to the sales environment for those willing to adapt. As today's Sales Maker, you can get in touch with your target market in a low cost (sometimes no cost) manner. But as discussed in previous chapters, it has also placed much more power in the hands of customers and professional buyers. Crucially, it has changed the way people buy, and has changed how sales professionals engage and communicate with the modern day buyer. In this chapter, we focus on how to use the power of the internet to build a better prospect database - a credible online presence that speaks the language that means something to your prospects. We also focus on how you can encourage those who are 'just looking' to come offline with you so that you can convert them into becoming paying customers. This is called the 'online to offline' sales conversion strategy.

Technology will continue to evolve and develop, and buyers will continue to use the latest tools and online platforms to communicate, learn and buy. From a selling perspective, you have two choices:

1. Embrace the change and adapt your own selling strategy so that it maximises the potential of technology.

2. Ignore the technological revolution and hope that things go back to the way they once were!

If you went for option 1, read on as you might find this chapter full of useful information because those who embrace technology are opening a door to a large range of selling styles and approaches that they have never used or tested before.

You can use technology to build a prospect database and get prospects coming to you – reducing your reliance on selling techniques such as cold calling to communicate with prospective buyers.

And, here's the challenge...

Using the internet as a lead generation tool has traditionally been the remit of the marketing department. The role of sales has been to follow up on leads generated by marketing. The success of sales professionals has traditionally been measured by the number of calls or sales visits made.

Technology is changing the rules. Today, sales professionals have far more control over how they and their products or services are marketed - and marketing departments now need to align themselves with sales. The two need to combine as a team so that they can work smarter, address the evolving challenges of the marketplace and ultimately drive increased sales results.

Some modern day, forward thinking sales organisations have already altered how they measure activity and have mutual sales and marketing KPIs and objectives.

We predict that this will be a major shift for most sales organisations in the coming years.

SO HOW DO YOU USE THE POWER OF THE INTERNET TO BUILD A DATABASE OF WARM PROSPECTS?

In previous chapters, we have covered how both buying and selling have changed as a result of technology and the internet. We also discussed the importance of having a credible online presence – meaning you need to provide today's educated customers with the information they want to see.

To establish what information and which media platforms you should be using online, you simply need to ask your customers where, when and how they prefer to buy and what level of information they would like to see online.

Ask the question, it really is as simple as that.

In the meantime, let us provide you with some fundamental online strategies that are relevant regardless of industry or sector.

THE THREE ONLINE FUNDAMENTALS

1. Target Market. Do you specialise in your customer's market or sector? Today's customers are sceptical; they fear making a wrong decision and they prefer to work with specialists rather than generalists. They LOVE working with experts – it means they don't have to think as much! There is some nice research to back this up: in a TED Talk posted in 2011, Noreena Hertz talked about the role of expertise in society. She said that brain scan measurements showed people's brainwaves flatline when they listened to an expert.

179

This means that if customers perceive you as an expert, their brain will literally switch off, and they will perceive what you are saying as being completely right. They put their brain and subsequently their decision making totally in your hands. If you specialise or have expertise in a particular market or industry then shout it from the hilltops, but do it online. Go to your selected websites or online forums and share what you know.

2. Messaging. The days of simply putting loads of product or service information online are over. This behaviour is known as 'feature dumping'; it's seller-centric messaging and not what today's customer wants to see. The message needs to change from being seller-centric to customer-centric and include the two things today's customers want to see: VALUE and RESULTS. This is where you use your value proposition which we covered earlier in the book. (See Chapter 3.)

3. Multimedia communication methods. Technological advancements mean today's buyer doesn't need to engage directly with a salesperson until they choose to. However, this doesn't mean you can't use multimedia platforms such as videos, webinars, social media and blogs as a way to build a better online relationship with your prospects. Encourage them indirectly to come offline and engage with you.

But remember, the vast array of multimedia platforms on offer can be overwhelming. It can be difficult to know which platform to choose. That confusion has forced lots of sales organisations to jump on the latest online bandwagon, only to end up disappointed with the results they achieve.

To select the right media platforms, start with the ones that your target market use and respond to.

The media platforms you select to use to engage and connect with your prospective buyer are heavily dependent on your target market and their communication habits. Some target markets will have a heavier reliance on LinkedIn, for instance, while some may use YouTube or Twitter.

IS 'SOCIAL PROOF' IMPORTANT IN YOUR 'ONLINE TO OFFLINE' SALES STRATEGY?

Social proof is all about finding out what others are doing, feeling validated by that, and choosing the same option. You only need to look at Trip Advisor to see the importance of social proof in today's market. Many people will not book a hotel or holiday without first checking the reviews on Trip Advisor. If you want to build customer trust and confidence in your product or service, it's very important that you include testimonials, case studies, video testimonials from customers and any other form of social proof, such as awards you have won or accreditations you have received.

Type your name into Google, go on...

Where you show up online also plays an important role in providing social proof. For example, if you run a Google search on your name or your company name, where are you showing up? Do you have a credible online presence? Do you have an up-to-date LinkedIn profile (more about this later)?

Many times, even if you search online for an email address, a LinkedIn account will come up first. People are reading yours, probably more regularly than you realise. Never underestimate the curiosity of today's buyers!

Insider Tip: Being a member of groups, associations, a regular blogger, and having a comment facility on your website will help you to build your social proof.

The key to getting prospects to engage with you offline is to make them an offer. Failing to provide an offer to engage is where so many sales organisations miss out on opportunities to sell. This is also why some believe an online sales strategy is very time-consuming and resource-heavy and produces very little in terms of results.

If you spend time, money and resources to get prospects to come online and review your company, products and services, you need to think of effective ways to move them offline, if your sales process supports that.

Many sales organisations fail to realise the importance of capturing the names and contact details of the people who visit their website. It's the equivalent of booking an expensive stand at an exhibition and then refusing to take visitors' business cards. Or going to a networking event and not taking note of the people who expressed an interest in your business. Every organisation should maximise their online return by capturing the contact details of all the people who visit their website. By providing simple offers to engage with customers, you can convert those who are simply looking (we like to call them 'suspects') into prospects or qualified prospects, who have made an informed decision to move further into the sales process with you. Then it's your job to turn those prospects into customers.

The keys are relevance, risk and reward. Your offer must be relevant to your target audience, and the first offer needs to be risk-free and must offer a reward or prize.

Simply having a phone number on your website and asking prospects to call you isn't enough anymore.

11 WAYS TO BEGIN MOVING RELATIONSHIPS FROM 'ONLINE TO OFFLINE'

1. Instant messenger, so visitors simply type their question and a live person responds in seconds
2. 'Call me' buttons
3. Instant Skype or video conferencing with a salesperson
4. Engage with Twitter, Facebook or LinkedIn
5. Offer free resources such as PDFs or audio interviews
6. No obligation instant quotes
7. Free trial
8. Live demo
9. Free consultation
10. Invitation for people to provide feedback or their opinion
11. A prominent phone number. (At Natural Training, we increased our incoming leads by 15% simply by making our phone number 30% larger on our website!)

By providing compelling value and adding risk-free offers to engage, you give your prospects and opportunity to get to know you a little better. It provides you, as the seller, with an opportunity to showcase your credibility and gives you an opportunity to build revenue!

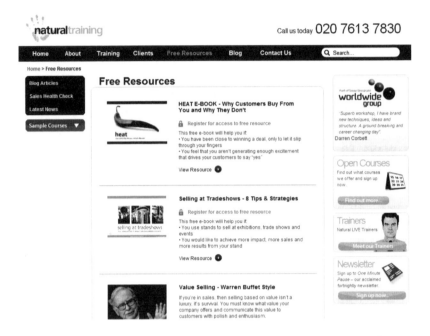

Fig 11.1: Free resources on the Natural Training website are among the most popular pages

HERE'S A GREAT EXAMPLE OF HOW THIS WORKS...

Natural Training recently won a very large six-figure training contract which came from an enquiry via our website. They saw we had a credible online presence, they downloaded a copy of our *HEAT* e-book, took a sales health check (which we offer as a free service) and then picked up the phone and called us. By that stage, they really felt that we knew what we were talking about and wanted to know more. (Having potential buyers come to you instead of you going to them is a real sign of just how powerful a credible online presence can be.) We were then invited to go in and pitch for the business. It took a lot of time and energy, but we won the deal.

What they didn't tell us until we won the deal is that we were up against six of the world's largest training organisations and that we were brought in as the wild card.

The objective of the training was to teach non-sales professionals to become proactive in generating opportunities online within their existing customer base. We won the deal based on our online presence and strategy to convert those who are 'just browsing' into paying customers. Of course, our proposal and strategy helped in winning the deal, but we had the opportunity to present to them because we have measures in place to move them offline.

Once you have built enough trust online with the modern day buyer, and you have provided a compelling offer for them to engage with you, you have the chance to build an even deeper relationship. You can demonstrate your expertise and showcase the value and results that prospects gain by becoming a customer with you. You can do this via email marketing, blogging, using social media sites or, if you have the right information, direct mail which is actually making a comeback.

Insider Tip: If you try to sell too quickly, you lose all the faith and trust that you have spent so much time building up.

When offline, provide them with information that adds value and makes them want more, just like you normally would.

Your 'online to offline' sales conversion strategy is a lot like dating! Apparently a large percentage of couples today meet online. Let's say, you found someone who you thought could be right for you so you made contact. Things seemed promising. Now, ask yourself how you'd feel if, after that first contact, your potential partner proposed to you. You'd probably run a mile. Well, that's exactly how today's modern buyer feels if you try to sell to them too quickly.

Like dating, here's what's important with online selling:
- ✓ Authenticity
- ✓ Respect
- ✓ Value
- ✓ Credibility
- ✓ Proof

When offline, provide them with information that adds value and makes them want more – just like you normally would.

The modern day 'online to offline' lead generation and sales conversion strategy

Online		Offline
Suspects	➜	Capture
Prospects	➜	Nurture
Customers	➜	Convert

As a final note, we have included a one-page Lead Generation and Marketing Plan that every modern day sales organisation can use. If you are a sales professional working within an organisation that hasn't yet embraced this online opportunity, please don't let this limit your success as there are lots of free resources online. Also, think about platforms like LinkedIn that provide you with the opportunity to generate your own leads and prospects.

Summary

- Technology has allowed low-cost leads to come into your organisation, but for most industries, you need to convert them to an offline relationship.
- Sales and marketing are starting to work together, which will grow as a trend significantly in the next three years.
- Social proof drives the need to establish both online and offline integrity.
- The modern Sales Maker adapts to the essential incorporation of online marketing within a sales role.
- There are crucial points you need for successful online engagement and selling – it's about establishing an authentic relationship, beyond the mouse!
- There are at least 13 ways to move from online to having a relationship, such as offering free, helpful business resources.
- Be calm, considered, and honest – the usual rules of natural human engagement apply.

TIME TO EVOLVE! YOUR SALES TOOLKIT:

- Study your company's website. Make a list of how many opportunities the customer has to engage with you offline. Can you see any new ways to move people from the internet into a relationship with you?
- Social proof as a concept is important to utilise in today's selling evolution. Dr Robert Cialdini wrote extensively about this in his book, *Influence: The Psychology of Persuasion*. Pick up a copy and work out how to weave 'social proof' through your next

customer experience.

- Download our free one-page Lead Generation and Marketing Plan to help you in this new era of 'online to offline' marketing. It contains everything you need to know to establish and grow a healthy, long term order book.
- Download our free e-book called *HEAT*. This e-book is all about maintaining a strong relationship with customers to keep the heat in the sale.
- Create your own 'online to offline' strategy and send it to one of our 'online to offline' expert coaches at Natural Training by emailing evolve@naturaltraining.com for a free critique.

To access the Natural Training sales resource centre for your 29 FREE resources, simply register online at www.naturaltraining.com/bonusresources

Chapter 12 - How to use LinkedIn as a lead generation tool

"To sell is to be human."
Matt Drought

Twenty years ago, you would be considered slightly mad if you told someone working in sales that you had a free resource that held details on most of the world's decision makers, informed you when they were promoted or moved to a new job, revealed who they knew and allowed you to get in touch with them at the click of a button. Today of course there is such a resource, and it's called LinkedIn. If you're not using LinkedIn as a sales tool, you need to read this chapter because it will help you to realise exactly why it's going to be your best friend.

Establishing a presence on LinkedIn starts with creating a personal profile. That takes minutes. Then you're in to the biggest online business networking site the internet has ever seen. If you work in sales, signing up to LinkedIn is the smartest move you'll make in a long time.

Why is it critical? Well, as Malcolm Gladwell would say, LinkedIn has reached a crucial "tipping point". More people in business are using it than not. And when you understand just how important it is to prepare for sales meetings and research customers or prospects, you start to understand this modern networking marvel.

And it works the other way too. As you introduce yourself to a prospect, they will undoubtedly turn their attention to LinkedIn in the hope of finding out more information about you.

Here are three key reasons for the modern day sales professional to be on LinkedIn:

1. It allows prospects to check out your profile. It's a great opportunity to sell yourself.
2. It's a great way to generate leads and to get in touch with key contacts that the gatekeepers always restrict you from reaching.
3. It allows you to research your prospects. You can get to know what their background is, who they know and even what books they are reading!

Insider Tip: Not being on LinkedIn is bad, but being on there and not providing any information is even worse. It's critical to sell yourself and your company effectively.

What about the figures?

HERE ARE SOME RATHER HEAD-TURNING ESTIMATES:

1. Right now in the UK, there are about 9.5 million active LinkedIn users.
2. Worldwide, LinkedIn has 175 million active users.
3. Usage worldwide is growing by a million per week.
4. In the UK, usage is growing by approximately 50,000 to 60,000 per month.

View LinkedIn's rapid growth live at: http://newin.LinkedIn.com/

GETTING THE PROFILE PAGE RIGHT!

LinkedIn is a combination of personal branding and corporate branding – both of which are crucial to you as a sales professional. You might have an incredible ability to build rapport, but you'll never get that across on a personal profile page. However, your company may be popular – and that's what gets you noticed. Alternatively, your positive activity within a group will bring your company to the attention of others.

The profile is the first place to start with LinkedIn, and it's crucial you get it right. When you come to write the profile, you are exposing both your personal side and your professional side. Be sure to take responsibility for both.

Insider Tip: It might be tempting to collaborate with the marketing department for help, but it's imperative that you write your own profile. Write it and get someone to read it. Remember to be authentic and natural.

Be sure to market yourself in a personally professional way. Avoid language you would use on the corporate website. When talking about the company or the products you sell, write it from a personal perspective. Talk about yourself and why you're passionate about what you do. There's nothing wrong with building a bit of a story...

HOW TO MAKE YOURSELF VISIBLE TO THE MOST PEOPLE ON LINKEDIN

- ➲ **Headline:** Always include your name in your headline (the bit below your name). This is always visible, and if someone outside your 'sphere' finds you via a keyword search, they will be able to

191

identify you immediately. Also, include some relevant keywords in this headline that will enable people to find you. For example, 'Business Improvement Consultant'.

➲ **Summary:** Write a clear and engaging summary of who you are and what you stand for. Remember, everyone else can see it! Be professional and clear about who you are and what you want to achieve.

➲ **Contact:** Where you have contact preferences, you'll notice there's a box where you can explain how best to get in touch with you. Use it! Again, this is for everyone to see. (See diagram, Fig 12.1: Make yourself more visible to others.)

THE PHOTO - STAYING HEAD AND SHOULDERS ABOVE THE COMPETITION

A photo on LinkedIn is essential. The reason is simple: it allows people to remember you. Like it or not, we all have features by which people can remember us – far better than they can a name.

These photos don't necessarily have to be professionally taken. Just ask a friend to take a close-up head and shoulders picture. It is worth remembering that if you're trying to link with someone and you don't have a picture, they will be more likely to ignore your request.

A DIFFERENT KIND OF SELLING...

By spending time on your profile and uploading an image of yourself, you are building your credibility on LinkedIn and removing barriers that could stop potential customers from trusting you. This is about social selling, which isn't sending out hundreds of messages to people trying to get them to buy your products. As we all know, that's bad enough via email!

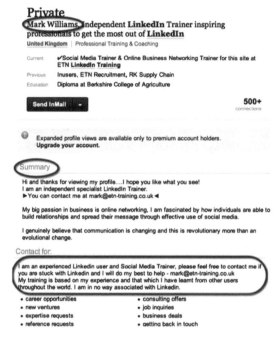

Fig 12.1: Make yourself more visible to others

Here are three tips to help you in the world of social selling:

1. It is a much better idea to market yourself on LinkedIn as a trusted advisor. You want to be the 'go-to' person, or the 'linchpin' as Seth Godin would say; someone people know, respect and think of as a source of quality information.

2. Interaction on social sites must be engagement-led so don't push for a meeting straight away. Offer

value and provide useful information or advice.

3. Help people out, and they will come to you for a meeting if they need one. It really is an environment of 'giver's gain' – the art of reciprocity is alive and well on LinkedIn!

A LinkedIn strategy to use today

Here are some of our best tips about using LinkedIn to drive sales:

- ✓ Understand who your prospects are and what they are interested in. You should know this already, but LinkedIn can help you get a more precise idea around job title and focus.
- ✓ Little and often is the key with LinkedIn. Ten minutes a day for a month will do more than sitting down for three hours on it once a month.
- ✓ Identify where you can source your information from. Who is active, who contributes to groups, and what can you contribute?
- ✓ Put in a process that consistently allows you to provide your prospects with the relevant information they need. For example, this might be setting an alarm once a week to find a resource and post it in a group.

LET'S LOOK AT A GREAT EXAMPLE THAT EXPLAINS THIS...

The smart way to use LinkedIn

In recruitment, consultants are constantly trying to connect with potential candidates in the industry they place into. Instead of connecting with everyone working within one industry, one smart consultant simply wrote three blogs related to the sector and shared links to read them all on his LinkedIn feed.

He asked experts from his target industry to give him feedback – and plenty did.

Then he started to post comments on news stories that were relevant to the industry, and more potential candidates commented. When he connected with the people who he knew would be great for the role he was filling, they were more than happy to connect (and have meetings offline) because he'd become the 'go-to' man in that industry.

THE COMPANY PAGE

Once static and fairly ineffective for the sales professional, today the company page allows status updates to targeted groups and offers an increased level of interaction. So, for example, if a company wanted to post a message to companies with less than 500 staff, it could by simply filtering its followers.

These pages have evolved into brochure sites, and when you consider the number of people on LinkedIn at any one time, getting them right is very important.

Within the company page, you can display your key products and services. You can include 'live links' to take visitors to another page where you have more space and availability to develop an understanding of products or services.

Insider Tip: You can even include videos here which can be very powerful engagement tools when you are trying to sell the key benefits of your product or service.

195

FOLLOW ME, I KNOW THE WAY!

"How do I get more followers on our company page?" is something we are asked a lot, so here is a very basic guide to building your network with high quality contacts...

Identify who you want to follow you. What do they value, what/who do they have an interest in, what are their movements on LinkedIn and what sort of groups do they join?

The best bait catches the nicest fish! Offer people incentives (competitions, exclusive news and updates) and reasons to follow you.

Market your page. Use plug-ins on your site and include links in your signature. Plug-ins refer to applications that give your LinkedIn page more of a feel of an interactive web-page.

In the example on the next page, Matt from Natural Training has the NT blog and a recommended reading list on his LinkedIn page. This enables the user to gain more of an insight into his activities and, as a result, the likelihood may increase of people wanting to do business with him. Other additions can include calendars, travel guides, Slideshare and your Twitter feed. To add more applications and features to your LinkedIn page, simply choose 'add sections' (see Fig 12.2) from the pop-up window.

LinkedIn as a lead generator

Does having hundreds of followers mean that you can use LinkedIn as an effective lead generation tool? Well, not necessarily. It does help though. Basically you, the sales professional, must work hard to build up your network. This really needs to become part of everyday working life. Each time you talk to a prospect, add them on LinkedIn. Very soon, your visibility will be growing at a rapid rate because the more direct contacts you have, the more you are exposed to other people's contacts. And so it goes on...

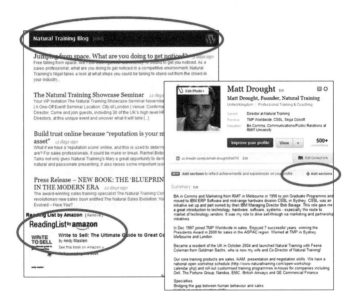

Fig 12.2: Add more applications and features to your LinkedIn profile

Insider Tip: In terms of lead generation, there is a tool called LinkedIn Signal. (See diagram 12.3) It allows you to search for words or phrases within updates. You can find updates from anyone on LinkedIn. Simply type in a key phrase. This identifies people who are interested in your field and then allows you to make connections or get the latest news which, in turn, you can 'feed' to your connections.

Once you have connected with your contacts, lead

generation on LinkedIn isn't really any different from lead generation anywhere else. You need to nurture leads, and brand yourself over time as the right option for their needs. You need to start discussions around their issues, and move them offline. (See Chapter 11 for information about how to do this.) You need to make them offers, and get them into a room with different influencers from your company.

The normal rules of selling still apply. For example, if you're too pushy from the start, you'll sabotage the entire relationship. Remember, engagement is the key to social selling. When sending an invite, make sure it's personalised; otherwise it's just seen as lazy and rude. Write a note that is short and concise. Once you're connected, you must resist the temptation to be too pushy. Once you have interacted a few times, perhaps then you can follow up with a request to meet.

Fig 12.3: Use LinkedIn Signal to make new connections or get the latest news

LinkedIn is the new form of connecting and an important way of getting in contact with people.

This isn't a platform for direct business results and 'instant sales' but it is a great networking tool.

LINKEDIN IS A MASSIVE ROOM FILLED WITH PEOPLE

Think of LinkedIn as a massive room filled with lots of people who you know through other people. Most of them have a big badge on, with more than their name – it also holds many other useful, personal particulars on it. Other people are there, but they are wearing masks, making it difficult to get to know them. In this big room, there are small groups of people who know each other very well, so you can't barge in and start conversations with them too easily. There are people who are wandering around with free gifts and prizes. There are people who are standing up speaking to small and large groups. There are people who look a bit lost. There are people who own companies, and there are people who deliver mail to companies.

So, while it's handy to have all of your contacts in the same room, you can see that they are in varying states of readiness to do business. You certainly won't be guaranteed any business – but it's your job to 'work the room' and begin or continue the sales process. Walking around saying "Do you want to buy what I have?" or "Do you want to meet up?" won't be effective in the room, as it won't be on LinkedIn. Apply your normal common sense and sales ability and you will prosper.

LinkedIn isn't a magic wand – it's very useful, but you need to work to keep your leads interested and therefore more

199

likely to convert. Having said that, it is a fabulous networking site. As a modern day sales professional, you must make sure you're using your time wisely, and LinkedIn is one tool that allows you to reach more people in a short space of time. Just be careful how you approach people and the kind of messages you send out. Those who get it right will unlock the door to incredible opportunities and brand new revenue streams. So, write that profile and get on board!

Seven more tips to use LinkedIn to drive sales

1. Assuming you don't know their name, finding people on LinkedIn is affected by how many relevant connections you have and how many relevant groups you join. Only first and second tier connections are fully visible with third tier and fellow group members being visible only by their surnames.
2. Identify active individuals – they are your key to a rich vein of contact expansion. Who is active, who contributes to groups, and what can you contribute in similar forums?
3. Put in a process that allows you to provide your prospects with the relevant information they need on a consistent basis. For example, this might be setting an alarm once a week to find a resource and post it in a group.
4. You can join up to 50 groups on LinkedIn, and it makes sense to do so for the visibility benefits we've just covered. However, we would advise you to be involved in just a few groups (discussions). The remainder of your groups should have the settings changed so that you do not receive any emails from them (or you will get overwhelmed!).

5. The advanced search function can be very effective. Simply enter those job titles that you feel are relevant by using a simple Boolean string such as; "ceo" OR "chief executive" OR "md" OR "managing director". Multiple words that you wish to be seen as a phrase need to be in speech marks (for example, "chief executive") and you should widen your options by thinking of as many relevant titles and variants separated by the OR command (must be in caps). In addition to this, you might wish to type in a postcode and specify a mileage radius of that postcode, for example, 35 miles from EC2.

6. Having built a list this way, you can then set about 'engaging' with them - this may be by contributing to a group discussion that they are involved in or by introducing yourself via an InMail (paid message) or a direct message to someone you share a group with (this is only possible when you are in the group). There are, of course, plenty of other ways to engage away from LinkedIn. Having engaged, the next step is to connect. Once they are a first tier connection, they will see your status updates, and you are able to send them a free direct message. Once a prospect is a connection, they can also be 'tagged', for example, hot prospect. In this way, LinkedIn works a bit like a Customer Relationship Management (CRM) system.

7. Finally, if you run events, seminars or open programmes and would like to invite your LinkedIn connections, simply use the free event facility to post your event and then share it with your connections and groups.

Summary

- LinkedIn is the pre-eminent online business networking tool that can make you money.
- There are vital and valid business reasons to be on LinkedIn: lead generation and research being key.
- Generating a list and building followers are two of the key milestones to making money from LinkedIn.
- It's important to maximise your profile page with tips, features and applications.
- Our 'little and often' technique will drive success for you on LinkedIn.
- Lead generation via LinkedIn includes segmenting a list and nurturing it.
- LinkedIn is a massive room filled with people – you still need to work the room!

TIME TO EVOLVE! YOUR SALES TOOLKIT:

- Watch LinkedIn expert Mark Williams talking about using LinkedIn more effectively: http://www.youtube.com/watch?v=-Iuzp0IHnwY.
- Commit to spending ten minutes on LinkedIn EVERY morning for the next 30 days and measure how it works.
- Become a member of three groups of like-minded people and contribute actively to the conversations.
- Post two short articles about a recent client, product or networking experience. Add in three applications and 'extras' on your LinkedIn profile to make it more attractive and useful for users.

To access the Natural Training sales resource centre for your 29 FREE resources, simply register online at www.naturaltraining.com/bonusresources

Chapter 13 - Referral selling - your modern day sales weapon

"Life is pretty simple: You do some stuff. Most fails. Some works. You do more of what works."
Tom Peters

As a consumer, you probably rely more on referrals than you think. On Amazon, at a click of a mouse, you can tell what 138 customers think of the new Garmin bike computer – because they have bought it and are using it. You probably trust those reviews more than the manufacturer's sales literature, right? From the viewpoint of today's Sales Maker, the referral is your dream, as you can cut out significant barriers to sale and go direct to the already-warm prospect. Imagine if there were a range of new ways to generate more referrals through your existing selling strategy. How much extra revenue could that create with minimal effort? In this chapter, we discuss the practical and logical steps involved in the art of gaining referrals.

There's nothing better than a referral - that incoming phone call on a quiet morning when your prospect list is looking as old and dusty as a first edition of *Moby Dick*. "Hello is that Nick? John Murphy recommended I give you a call, Nick. I'm very interested in the services you provide and getting the same results as John did. Can you talk now?"

How good is that? Someone asks for you by name, and already wants to do business with you. They are asking for your time! They are being polite, and eager. Sigh. Sales nirvana!

Essentially, what you have just done is to skip past all the awkward questions and feelings in the initial stages of the sales cycle that prevent us from selling, such as:

- "Do I know you?"
- "Do I trust you?"
- "I already don't like you!"
- "I'm better than you."

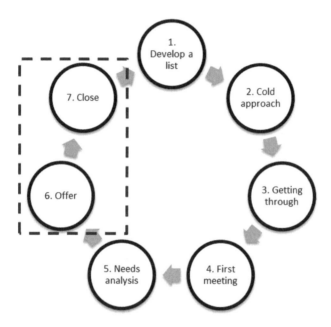

Fig 13.1: Use referral selling to accelerate the sales cycle to the final stages. Beautiful!

Just consider for a moment how easy life could become by using referrals as your modern sales strategy.

Here are the top five advantages:

1. Identifying new prospects
2. Saving time

3.   Generating instant trust
4.   A smoother, more confident sale
5.   Avoiding the competition

The only problem is, referrals are rare. Imagine if you could manufacture the referral process and take control of this area of your selling strategy to the point where you could rely on referral business on a regular basis. How would that impact your sales targets?

The good news is you can, and with the traditional methods of selling (door knocking and cold calling, for instance) having less impact, now is the perfect time. You just need to nail your referral strategy!

Essentially, the way to gain referrals falls into two broad categories: direct and indirect.

1.   DIRECT. DON'T ASK, DON'T GET.

In sales, it is very easy to overcomplicate and overwork things in our mind as we prepare for conversations. However sometimes keeping it simple is the best policy. In terms of referrals, this means asking a simple, direct question: "Do you know anyone who may like to use our services?"

Salespeople have a strange fear of asking direct questions, but the truth is, the simplest way to ensure clients refer you is to be direct! It won't always be the right solution, but it's important not to overcomplicate things.

A GREAT EXAMPLE OF DIRECT QUESTIONING FROM PAUL...

A few years ago, I booked a taxi to take me to the airport,

and the driver picked me up from outside my house. "Nice house," he said. "How much did you pay for it?" I told him, and he asked, "Cash or mortgage?" Again, I told him. It struck me that although I'm not necessarily comfortable answering those kinds of questions, it didn't stop me from answering. In fact, the entire journey was taken up discussing my home purchase. Along the way, I remember thinking that the driver needed to learn some diplomacy. But it also reminded me that when you ask a direct question, people will answer you.

Often when it comes to client referrals, people just don't ask that key question. It's an invisible barrier that in sales you need to overcome. Take comfort in the fact that being a sales professional who asks for referrals requires no skill or specific training – it's about making a habitual change, not a skill change. **Put simply, you need to get into the habit of asking for referrals.**

Entrepreneur and star of *Dragons' Den*, James Caan, recommends that you take your direct question one step further and actually be more specific. He claims he always ask for a particular number of referrals. I would support that, as I think there can be too many woolly questions in the sales process.

Here's how they compare:

1. "Do you know anyone who could use our services?"
2. "Can you please give me three names of people who you know would benefit from the services we provide?"

Which option do you think would offer a better response?

The second one, of course. The first gives an open invitation to answer: "Oh, okay, I'll have a think about it." This is of no use to you because all you'll end up doing is badgering the client about referrals. The second question is focused. If you want something, you have to ask for it – politely of course. People might only give you two referrals, which might be 100% more than they would have done if you had asked a general question.

The point with this type of referral selling is to be direct, specific and persistent.

ARE YOU USING YOUR CLOSING TECHNIQUES WITH REFERRALS?

Within this direct questioning, it's important to ask for a referral in a way that makes it a closing question. Remember, you're looking to seal a deal – one that will make you money! So treat it as a mini sale.

The deal is to get hot leads via a customer. You will be better positioned to do that when you have recapped the value to someone – in the same way that you would close any other sales conversation.

One element that's particularly useful here is getting people to talk about why they liked or enjoyed the service or product you provided. It warms up the referral, in the same way that you will warm up the close.

Here are some useful questions to consider when you take this approach to gaining referrals:

1. What was it specifically that you liked about our service?

2. How has it changed your life or working environment?
3. What has been the impact on the bottom line/your team/your environment?

Your focus should be on encouraging your customer to talk about the benefits of the service before you ask for the referral – get them enthused about the work you've been doing. All you're really doing is putting the customer in the right mindset to say, "Yes I know a few people who could use this".

Without using closing techniques to get that referral it can be cold. The direct approach is still a key element, but people are far more likely to respond positively once they have spent 90 seconds saying how great you are. Psychologists call it 'mental conditioning' – helping the mind become predisposed to an environment by putting them back in the moment.

Insider Tip: Ask your customers to ring up their contacts direct for you – it's stronger that way. They can even bring you into a conference call or meet up together at an industry event for coffee.

CONSIDER THIS SITUATION...

A training company wants to develop its customer base in the automotive industry, and currently has one major client. The training company provides training sessions across a three-month period and, at the end of each period, meets with the company decision makers to assess results and discuss reports. The results are always positive.

When is the optimum time to launch that direct question and request a referral?

1. After the first month of work, when the company is happy with the initial roll out and has seen some positive results?
2. Midway through the first three-month period because the company has had a good taste for the kind of work the training company provides and has seen a return on investment?
3. At the end of the first three-month period, during a focused meeting when the training company has just reported back figures for investment return and has received a glowing response from the client?

By taking the third option, you are effectively putting yourself in the strongest position to request a referral from this client. Why? Because not only has the work been positive and shown a return, you are capitalising on a period of time when the client sees your service in a positive light.

2. INDIRECT: HELPING PEOPLE TO THINK DIFFERENTLY.

Unlike the direct approach, the indirect referral request represents a whole range of alternative routes – all of which arrive at the same destination: solid and effective referrals. The idea behind this approach is to put steps in place that help people think differently about you, your brand and your service.

The indirect referral is the big growth area in referral selling. Just ask Facebook's Mark Zuckerberg! Facebook now uses your endorsements to sell third party products. Press 'like' on Goodyear tyres? Then expect your face to be part of an ad selling tyres to your friends. One of our great clients at

Natural Training is a prominent London-based real estate agency - it receives more leads via Facebook than any other means! And it's free!

Fig 13.2: Brands like Lego use customers as a referral network on Facebook

Right now, companies across the world are asking customers to like them, recommend them, blog about them, poke them, write songs about them and gather a flash mob for them. This is all indirect referral selling – it's big, it's real and various versions of it will help drive leads to you and make you money.

HERE'S AN EXAMPLE FROM PAUL...

Two weeks ago, I was sitting at the kitchen table, watching my young kids think of various creative angles to win a Nintendo DS in their latest competition. They had to find a code, buy a game, match the code to some other thing in the game, go online, input the code and probably about another ten things that I didn't understand, but they loved.

Initially, I was angry that a corporation was brainwashing my kids. Then I realised it's no different to what I used to do - they are simply being caught up in a slightly more evolved indirect referral programme!

When I was a kid, I remember sitting at dinner one day and reading details of a competition on the back of a Heinz Tomato Ketchup bottle (my brother had it on everything so it was a permanent fixture on the table). I was staring at it thinking, "We need to enter this, because all we have to do is write 30 words why we like it so much." Simple. So we did and guess what? We won. The prize was a huge supply of Tomato Ketchup!

So, what's the relevance here? At the time, I couldn't work out why they would be giving all that amazing Tomato Ketchup away, but it was about changing the way we thought about the brand.

We were tasked with really thinking about the words we would use to describe Tomato Ketchup – because we only had 30 words and it had to go on the back of the label! Then we went to find an envelope and write the address. Then we went to the post office, got a stamp and sent it off. Commitment, perseverance, loyalty – all for a bottle of sauce!

Heinz managed to turn us from normal consumers of their product into champions. No prizes for guessing what my brother and I talked about to friends for months afterwards. I still remember it like it was yesterday!

The important take away here is that Heinz shifted the way we interacted with the brand – and we couldn't wait to tell (or refer) as many people as we could.

Many companies make use of indirect referrals to get the same response – they want customers to champion their work and share their passion with others. That's when they truly work.

Your own indirect referral scheme – case studies

In sales, you probably can't impact the way your company goes to market, presents the brand on LinkedIn or Facebook, or becomes viral on Twitter. (No harm to suggest it, but you have selling to do, right?) So you need to work out your own low cost techniques, and case studies are perfect for this.

THE WRITTEN CASE STUDY

Case studies are stories about how customers have benefited from hanging out with you. Most of the case studies we see at Natural Training are boring, outdated, and a bit insincere. These need a fresh look, especially if they are to generate the kind of referral results that we have been talking about already in this chapter.

Just as Heinz did so brilliantly, companies need to let their customers own the case study and drive the content.

HERE'S A GREAT EXAMPLE OF HOW TO GET THE CASE STUDY RIGHT...

To illustrate the point, let's look at two different companies and focus on how they generate content for their case studies. Both companies appreciate the importance of case studies in generating referral work, and both have an excellent working relationship with customers.

Company 1 uses case studies in all of its proposals and is keen to secure a bank of fresh testimonials for a range of new clients. To save time and to avoid heaping unnecessary pressure on customers, it decides to write up the case study internally, covering the main points of the work completed, and then simply ask for client sign off. The clients sign off every time – most of them don't even read it as they trust the company entirely.

Company 2 takes a different approach. The marketing team builds a monthly online magazine that reviews industry updates, best practice, latest offers, messages from the CEO, and plenty more. The company approaches one of its best clients and asks if they would like to feature in the magazine with a double page spread. The customer accepts. The company sends a photographer to the customer and even a professional writer to interview and help them get their message across about working with them and the kind of results they have achieved together. The magazine is published, and the customer feels an enormous sense of pride in their involvement and ownership of the article. Two different approaches, but essentially two case studies created. In terms of referrals, the best case study will be championed by the customer – enjoyed and shared among potential prospects for the company.

Company 1 has little chance of their case study being shared on social sites or emailed to contacts – it's functional, but won't have the sort of emotional impact needed to circumnavigate the customer globe.

Company 2, on the other hand, knows that the customer loved the case study and will be more than happy to send it around to show as many people as possible. Why? Because the customer owns the case study. If sales professionals can collaborate with customers (rather than spoon feeding them), these case studies will become hugely important in terms of referral work and driving fresh opportunities.

Insider Tip: Make your case studies and testimonials customer-centric as opposed to making them all about your company.

VIDEO CASE STUDIES

A 'talking head' has always worked well. Potential customers can see real customers express their emotion and expose their natural style – words on a page really can't achieve this. The difference with today's modern selling evolution is that you can share it so easily and if it's good, you won't even have to try! It may grow wings and take off, propagating around the world via all the social media platforms.

The problem is some customers won't like the idea of being in front of a camera – particularly when they're not necessarily getting anything in return.

How to get around this:
- ✓ Encourage them to talk in a natural conversation
- ✓ Create a natural roundtable discussion with free-flowing conversation
- ✓ Take the camera away and record a podcast

The key to the success of this kind of indirect referral work lies in helping the client to feel good about themselves. And, perhaps even more importantly, look good.

It is far more likely that customers will forward a video of themselves on to their own contacts if it is well-produced with strong and professional branding and appearance. Ultimately, just as with the case study, the secret is to make the client feel as though it's all about them.

Summary

- The sales world is evolving into a climate of referral selling. Don't get left behind!
- Referral selling is a beautiful way to generate quality leads.
- Referral selling accelerates you through the sales cycle towards the close, removing specific prospecting barriers.
- Both direct and indirect referral selling are successful – try to achieve a balance of both.
- Sometimes timing is everything when it comes to referral selling.
- Help customers take ownership of case studies – customer-centric wins every time.

TIME TO EVOLVE! YOUR SALES TOOLKIT:

- Download a sample client case study template to help you structure your customer referrals and proof.
- Resolve to ask EVERY customer for three key contacts for you to call – this should become an on-going behaviour for you from today!
- Be alert to how other companies are cashing in on the indirect referral scheme phenomenon. Notice how customers get involved in their brands then adapt their ideas, and use whatever low cost ways you can to spread your customer message.

- Resolve to spend ten minutes per week looking at what your competitors are doing to encourage referral selling.

To access the Natural Training sales resource centre for your 29 FREE resources, simply register online at www.naturaltraining.com/bonusresources

Chapter 14 - Develop the mindset of a modern day sales professional

"If your lifeguard duties were as good as your singing, a lot of people would be drowning."
Simon Cowell

Selling is evolving around you. To be successful, you need to adapt your processes, strategies and approach. But most of all, you have to adapt your mind. The requirements of today's Sales Makers are far different from a few years ago. To hit targets consistently and generate new revenue streams, it is vital that you have the right mindset for the job. In this chapter, we look at what makes the 'best of the best' in sales with a focus on what you could be doing differently to transform results.

What are some of the key attributes that top performers in today's sales environment have in common?

1. Top performers are authentic and natural in their approach.
2. Top performers are clear about their own motivations.
3. Top performers are able to make a connection with customers that helps them to stand apart.
4. Top performers are equipped to drive a sale.

There is one attribute that runs through each of these and without it, the sales professional will simply fall short of targets every single time. That attribute is a positive mindset, or attitude.

HIRE ON EXPERIENCE – FIRE ON ATTITUDE

When recruiters recruit salespeople, they tend to look through CVs and spot relevant knowledge and skills. Thus, they hire based on experience. Yet they tend to fire salespeople on attitude (experience doesn't matter when firing). Is this a sensible approach? Or should recruiters start reversing this trend? When you see this brought to life in the graphic below, it's easy to see that it's the attitude that drives the acquisition of skills, knowledge and experience. So really, recruiters should be hiring on attitude and firing on skills, not the other way around!

Fig 14.1: Attitude drives skills and experience

Away from sales for a second; whenever you watch a major sporting event the camera will pan across the players just before the game starts. No doubt you'll have noticed that each player will have their own way of preparing. Some stare at the ground, others slap themselves across the face. Others recite motivational sayings and words to themselves. The rituals in which these individuals prepare vary greatly, but the end goal is the same; to focus the mind.

How has the winning sales mindset evolved?

Traditionally, the mindset has been all about how salespeople feel about themselves. For example, one American sales guru used to encourage salespeople in their car to look at themselves in the rear vision mirror and call out "I like myself, I like myself..." over and over.

This might have some superficial effect, but the successful salesperson today has to think much more about the mindset that they bring to conversations and meetings. The winning mindset today has to be about dealing with the frustration arising from customers' changing workloads, roles and environment. There is much more variation, complexity and stress in the workplace today, due mainly to company cutbacks and emerging technologies. Gone are the days when customers sat at their desks and were willing to take a call! Selling is not impossible – but it does take a creative, positive and energetic mind to stay on top time after time. And a thick skin!

PERFORMANCE MATTERS AS MUCH AS EVER

Sales is about performance, and the high performers are those who have the mental strength and focus to be able to handle and manage the job at hand. That could mean prospecting, hitting targets or closing a deal. Either way, mindset and attitude are often what sets today's sales elite apart from traditional sales professionals. We don't often give our mind the attention it deserves. Think of your mindset as something external, like an attractive piece of clothing. Like it or not, you're wearing your mindset every day, just like your clothes. It affects the way you behave. So would you rather people see a positive salesperson, or a negative one? It's your mindset that drives behaviour - that's what your customer sees in you.

Insider Tip: In sales, we talk extensively about making the customer feel good, relaxed and at ease. Want to know the best way to make someone feel nervous, tense and negative before you even open your mouth? Look and feel negative!

TWO TECHNIQUES TO SHIFT YOUR THINKING TO POSITIVE

1. Visualisation:

Ever caught yourself imagining how well a meeting is going to go, or speaking aloud in conversations that haven't happened? We all visualise in business - it helps us to prepare naturally for an event. However, like a muscle, you can develop this talent to become a stronger part of your routine. Just like an athlete, you can use visualisation to focus - to see and hear the kind of success levels that you want to achieve. What does success actually look like? Play it back in your mind and keep reminding yourself of it. Perhaps success has looked like increased profits and commission pay in the past, and that meant a weekend away or tickets to an exciting event. Be very specific.

2. Language:

If you're constantly using negative words to describe yourself, your company or your performance, that negativity will feed into your behaviour. Think of the most positive periods in your career and the kind of words you use to describe them. Make sure they are the words that enter your mind when you think about the work schedule you are facing and the challenges ahead.

You can switch your entire mindset and behaviour by changing the words you use to describe your life.

HERE'S AN EXAMPLE...

One of our advertising clients decided to hold a meeting for the eight members of its Board. They wanted to discuss the type of language they were using. They isolated the negative words they were using in front of their teams, and then made a list of more positive words. They all made a commitment to each other to try for one month to use these positive words and phrases in their conversations, emails and communication.

The results were really encouraging – not only did the mood of the place lift palpably, but the staff started to use more positive language as well! The advertising agency realised that positive language is infectious – as is the type of mood they generate, and now the Board meets more regularly to discuss how to sustain the new energetic culture.

This entire book is focused on the modern day sales environment and how the modern day salesperson should be adapting their approach to accommodate the change. Even though the contents of the new approach to selling (value selling, building rapport, becoming a Sales Maker) are important, so too is the ability to make changes where necessary. This is precisely what is required when we talk about shifting mindset to a positive framework.

HERE'S A GREAT EXERCISE TO TRY...

The visualisation exercise

In the left column of the following table, write down FIVE occasions where you have unearthed a new opportunity and enjoyed success from your hard work, aptitude and commitment. In the right column, write down either how it made you feel or what you rewarded yourself with as a result.

Success Story	Reward
Hitting targets	*Spontaneous weekend to Spain with the family.*

Work hard at visualising these stories and rewards on a regular basis to encourage a more positive mindset.

It's crucial to think about your personal achievements: sales targets are great, but to be truly inspired by them and to use them to drive a positive frame of mind, you need to understand what it means to you. Remember, you're far more likely to perform at your optimum when excited on a personal level.

HOW TO BREAK THE HABIT OF A LIFETIME

Sometimes making this shift in mindset can be easy to talk about but slightly harder to achieve, especially when we're talking about changing our entire outlook. For many sales professionals, it's not a case of focusing on some positive experiences - it takes time and effort to make the all-important switch.

It might make it easier to think about making changes in your life by first understanding how much you step out of your comfort zone at the moment. Sometimes, we might think we're brave and constantly looking for new opportunities and ways to change or adapt, but the reality is we never leave the area where we're most content.

HERE'S AN EXAMPLE...

Comfort zones can be hard to spot. A journalist I once knew had climbed his way to a senior role at a magazine before the age of 30, which was an impressive achievement at the time. He had real promise and the publishing firm had high expectations of him. Problem was he'd found his comfort zone.

Ten years down the track guess what he's doing? That's right, same job, same magazine. He's good at what he does, so the magazine will never get rid of him. After all that early promise, what could he be doing now if he'd had the courage to stretch his comfort zone?

To make sure you don't fall into the same trap, use the following steps to make those positive changes:

➲ Think about and decide what it is you want to change. Let's assume it's something like asking highly effective sales questions.

➲ Accept the fact that you can't become the 'world's greatest' instantly! Break your goals down into smaller, more achievable milestones to give yourself a greater chance.

➲ Think about your last few sales. Where might you have asked more effective questions?

➲ Be honest with yourself. Work out what is working and what is not working. Ask for feedback from customers and colleagues.

➲ Use a simple score sheet to improve your performance at each sales meeting you attend, which will drive continual improvement.

When we talk about zones and stretching yourself to change habits and develop ability as a sales professional, there are three key areas to consider:

1.   **The comfort zone.** Here you do the same things over and over again and wonder why they don't generate better results in today's market.

2.   **The stretch zone.** This is where you'll make it in today's modern selling environment – always keen to sacrifice comfort for new experiences and learning.

3.   **The panic zone.** No-one wants to be here. It's where you feel constantly worried that the company is making cutbacks and fear for your job.

ARE YOU IN A COMFORT ZONE?

As is the case with the aforementioned journalist, we find our comfort zone and refuse to step out of it. This isn't good enough in the modern sales environment because the rapid pace of change means we have to adapt and develop all the time just to keep up. We see it all the time: despondent salespeople who "didn't see it coming". The reality is, the current rate of change means there will be more negative salespeople – unless attitudes change first! Giving yourself opportunities to get out of that comfort zone will (believe it or not) expand the zone and make it easier to break existing habits.

For starters, just get into the habit of breaking habits.

So, even if you need to travel the same way every day, just try something different for no other reason than it's different.

HERE'S A GREAT EXERCISE...

Think about the terms 'comfort zone', 'stretch zone', and 'panic zone'. What words do you associate with each zone? What can you do to move the words from the panic zone to the stretch zone? Write them down and start to think about how you can go about achieving them, step by step.

This again comes back to attitude and anyone in sales who isn't willing to learn and step out of their comfort zone once in a while will never outperform those who do.

THE UNIVERSITY OF ME – WHAT ARE YOU GRADUATING IN THIS WEEK?

When we talk about the University of Me, we are referring to a sales professional's willingness to be constantly learning and developing his or her understanding of key concepts, ideas, products and services. Basically, anything that will better their performance.

How are you taking responsibility for your learning today? Some salespeople will wait around for their employer to send them on a training programme; others will make use of a large variety of free resources and others will seek to be tutored by more experienced and talented heads around them.

Here are some quick tips on how you can graduate from the University of Me...

- ✓ **Invest in yourself.** Make time for learning and development. In sales, you're the difference between hitting targets and not hitting targets so keep yourself in optimum form by constantly learning. Knowledge is at your fingertips.
- ✓ **Take responsibility for your own success.** Don't wait for your employer to invest in your training. Take it on yourself! Ten years down the track, if you want to be working somewhere else and making 500% more money, ask yourself this: Will one training day a year from my company help me to achieve that? No, probably not.
- ✓ **Be willing to change.** The most successful sales professionals are learning all the time and show an absolute dedication to changing. The environment you operate in is always changing, so accept that knowledge and new skills are the best way to stay on top of that change.
- ✓ **Ask for feedback.** The University of Me isn't just

about going onto the internet and reading guides or relevant articles; it's also about asking powerful questions of those around you and acting on feedback. If you have the right attitude to developing skills and knowledge, you'll accept the feedback no matter whether it's negative, positive or indifferent.

In this chapter, we've focused our attention on change and how it is so important for salespeople to have a positive mindset when it comes to adapting to the new selling environment.

The most important point is that high-performers have a positive mindset. What they don't do is allow themselves to focus attention on things that can't be changed. If they did, they would never develop or improve because they'd be fighting a losing battle.

Pick your fights wisely and only ever focus on the things you can change.

We will leave the last word with Steve Jobs. It is a passage from his official biography by Walter Isaacson, and it sums up the passion you need in today's market to sell and prosper:

"The older I get, the more I see how much motivations matter. The Zune (digital music player) was crappy because the people at Microsoft don't really love music or art the way we do. We won because we personally love music. We made the iPod for ourselves, and when you're doing something for yourself, or your best friend or family, you're not going to 'cheese out.'

If you don't love something, you're not going to go the extra mile, work the extra weekend, challenge the status quo as much.

Summary

- Top performers are authentic, clear, great at making a real connection with people, and equipped to make a sale.
- This is all bound together by a positive mindset: the attitude that drives selling behaviours.
- Selling has changed: it now requires a creative, positive and energetic mind (and thick skin!).
- Gaining a positive mindset is possible using visualisation and language.
- Breaking old habits and moving out of comfort zones are both critical elements of top performers.
- We discussed the University of Me and having the right attitude to dedicate yourself to a lifelong learning cycle!

TIME TO EVOLVE! YOUR SALES TOOLKIT:

- Download our Performance Mindset worksheet to fine-tune your own selling attitude for today's natural selling evolution.
- Resolve to spend one hour a week consuming the finest sales information in the market. Download our 21 Recommended Resources Sheets to get a head start.

To access the Natural Training sales resource centre for your 29 FREE resources, simply register online at www.naturaltraining.com/bonusresources

Over to you: turning ideas into habits

**"In this very real world, good doesn't drive out evil.
Evil doesn't drive out good. But the energetic
displaces the passive."**
Bill Bernbach

As a sales professional, you have 40-60 hours in a working week to dedicate to making money and being successful. If you have read this book, you now have a new repertoire of ideas to help you do so. Your head is probably swimming with new possibilities!

We have all read books and been temporarily inspired, only to let the ideas fall by the wayside as we get busy, returning to the same habits. Please don't let this be the case – the time to create a roadmap to revenue is now!

Maybe you have circled some of the ideas, or written them down in a to-do list. Whatever your system for recording new ideas, it's crucial that you start putting some of them into action in the next few days. To move ideas into habits is a rare talent in society, but the people who are able to do this on a regular basis are some of the most highly paid individuals on earth.

The key with habits is to begin by diarising them, putting the best strategies into online diaries such as Outlook, and setting reminders. For example, if one of your actions is to use our Value Generator tool, then you need to use it three or four times over the next month to turn it into a habit. Then it moves from something that feels unnatural and new to something that is second-nature and habitual.

Don't get left behind. The sales world is evolving. Change with it and reap the rewards.

Thank you for reading the book and for investing in yourself.

Good luck in your journey.

THE 21 NATURAL SALES LAWS

1. Your communication needs to be clear and memorable.
2. You don't get a second chance to make a good first impression.
3. Everything you do is open for critique by customers – your reputation is everything.
4. Don't say "Blah blah" when "Blah" will do.
5. Know your value and speak it at every opportunity.
6. The best time to make a sale is when you have just made one.
7. Spend more time on what makes you money.
8. Unmet need is central to every sale.
9. A referral from an existing customer is ten times more powerful than a referral from you.
10. People buy from people they trust.
11. Stay positive by avoiding those who aren't.
12. Customers have egos – appeal to theirs.
13. Plan tomorrow today, not tomorrow.
14. Be bold – no-one is going to call the 'Sales Police'.
15. A good salesperson will make a customer feel good about the product, but a great salesperson will make customers feel great about themselves.
16. Know your natural style and how to use it to your advantage.
17. Status is important – maintain equal or slightly less status than your customer.
18. Don't leave your personality at the door.
19. Never lie or argue with a customer.
20. Selling is testing and playing – treat it with humour.
21. Be creative in your efforts; doing things the same way as always may be a flawed strategy.

About Natural Training

WWW.NATURALTRAINING.COM – EST. 2005

Natural Training started trading in 2005 with a simple proposition: fresh, relevant, practical training that works with your natural personality rather than training which crunches against it. We simply add some tools and concepts that help rather than constrict natural style.

Based in London and servicing the world, Natural Training focuses on delivering group workshops and personal coaching to big name brands representing most industry sectors. A key focus is sales training with a customer-centric approach that has evolved to meet the needs of today's market.

Formed by Matt Drought, formerly of TMP Worldwide, and Feena Coleman, formerly of Goldman Sachs, Natural Training now has over 2,500 clients enjoying our practical, results driven training.

Natural Training has 20 staff maintaining our superb customer experience including 15 trainers who have been selected from a pool of over a thousand applicants over eight years.

NATIONAL TRAINING AWARD – 2010

Natural Training won the award in the 'Providing Education and Training' category at the National Training Awards (NTA) at the central London regional ceremony in 2010 for a sales training programme provided to the world's seventh largest technology company, EMC. The award recognised the innovative way in which Natural Training drove positive selling behaviours throughout EMC's partner and distributor network resulting in real financial gains. The training helped to drive new business into EMC's pipeline, and registered an industry-leading 400:1 ROI.

Founder of Natural Training, Matt Drought says: "It is such a pleasure to be recognised by the training industry with this award, as the NTA brings with it the finest reputation. We built a pioneering training programme that swept through the entire EMC organisation including their Reseller and Distribution network, changing the behaviours of Inside and Field Sales teams, and Sales Management. The process of due diligence that the NTA went through was extraordinary, in order to prove that we helped EMC build a substantial new business pipeline through the depths of the recession."

However, the most dramatic result of the training was the rapid acceleration past the project's initial targets with £48 million of opportunity being opened on the training days alone.

BEST GLOBAL TRAINING PROGRAMME– 2011

Dell Computers and Natural Training won the 'Best Training Programme 2011' at the prestigious Golden Peacock Global Training Awards for a revolutionary

Customer Mindset Training Programme.

Natural Training's Design Team created the training programme with a focus on developing empathy within call centre customer care, technical and sales environments. The highly interactive programme combines use of technology and blended learning techniques, aimed at developing a greater sense of rapport, moving trainees out of 'automated customer mode' into a warm human interaction.

The Award recognised the following attributes of the programme:

- A full-day training investment driving exceptional Customer Experience
- A collaboration programme between Sales and Support training organisations
- Innovative approach to learning – interactive and experiential
- Large scale deployment – 17k employees trained over three quarters
- Tracking impact results on Communication NPS (PESurveys) of 11% in Sales and 5% in Services

What our clients say about working with us ....

"Looked at how I can make it as easy as possible for our customers to do business with us."
  Glen Anderson, Business Development Manager, Fujifilm

"We have worked beautifully together to design a programme that suits our target diverse audience. The training is rich in content and aligns to our capability framework."
  Judy Goldberg, L+D Director, Discovery Channel

"Absolutely brilliant. I feel a lot more confident in calling customers now. It gave me more confidence and got me thinking about new reasons to engage directly with customers. I would recommend this training 100% - the NT team are lovely to deal with and really encourage you to outshine yourself. Thank you for a great day!"
  Nicola Roche, OEM EMEA Inside Sales Account Manager, Dell

"Excellent. Fantastic 'back to basics' Sales training. 110 customer meetings arranged and a team that is clearly more confident in proactive selling! Well worth the investment and time!!!"
  Mark Scanlan, Manager, Dell

"Extremely productive, enjoyable and very valuable – we unearthed 31 new opportunities in a single day with Natural Training where previous efforts had yielded only three. It's a great way for the Channel Development Managers to work closely with Reseller teams to help them build confidence in articulating the

Dell messaging and for us to get that message across to their customers to generate new opportunities – a real win-win situation for all."

Jo Hall, Channel Development Manager, Dell

"This training is beneficial; it makes a lot of sense. It was like a Eureka moment."

Kenny Reynold, Creative, Sky Television

"We have won 75% of our pitches since doing the course."

Andy Bell, Managing Director, Mint Digital

"It is worth noting that we have just had our best Sales Quarter ever and September was the best sold month ever. For the part you undoubtedly played in that, I thank you."

David Davies, Sales Director, Firebrand

"Given that we had set a very challenging stretch target of 22 new qualified appointments for the day, I was extremely impressed when the team finished the day on 29 appointments – far greater than any of us expected. Not only have we posted some impressive figures on the first day of the focus week, but the team is energised by the success, they are articulating the EMC messaging well and opening up some great conversations with clients on an enterprise level. This great start has meant the entire week has got off on the right note with the Insight team firing on all cylinders."

John Shean, Partner Account Manager, EMC

"An excellent course for achieving results. We achieved well above my expectations! Thanks for working with my team, recognising how they work and supporting them in a way that encouraged and energised them to listen and learn through the training sessions and implement their new skills right away on their calls with a great deal of very evident success. Natural Training really made

the difference to what typical vendor call out days can be."
David Vallance, Sales Manager, Insight

"It's no exaggeration to say I was stunned at the success we achieved, thank you for organising Natural Training."
Stuart Warner, Sales Manager, 2E2

"I felt like the training was running through my blood at the end."
Richard Coles, Monster.com

Contributors

Matt Drought

Fiona Challis

Greg Keen

James Marshall

Mark Williams

Fred Robson

Contributors

Mark Fineman

Deborah Sowry

Pat Upton

Paul Owen

Sally Glover

Sean Sidney